Getting Started With Computer Networking

A Practical Guide By:

Peter T. Paskowsky

Introduction

I began writing this book as an introduction to the world of networking for new Network Engineers. After a few years on the job, I wanted to compile all of my notes, thoughts, and knowledge in a form that could help out others just starting their careers.

I entered my first job with a certain degree of confidence in my knowledge from taking multiple Cisco exams and perhaps an even greater amount of humility about what I didn't know. This work is dedicated to the new guy on the job.

It's intended as a hand reference to double check what's been done and to provide helpful hints and advice on how to solve typical problems. It's aiming to cover the topics on the exams that I found critical in my career, and especially covering the things the exams never prepared me for. It assumes some knowledge of basic networking concepts such as IPv4 addressing, subnetting, and the OSI model.

The goal is to present this information in an accessible and easy to understand manner, in contrast with other sources such as exam study material or Cisco documentation. It can be used as a reference for code examples, or read cover to cover to familiarize yourself with many topics.

Included are many practical labs and configuration examples. I encourage you to build them out, test them, and expand upon them to increase your knowledge.

The book is loosely organised into sections covering basic configuration, managing routers and switches, advanced configurations, switching, routing, WAN technologies, and security concepts. Feel free to jump to those you are most interested in or find most useful.

I hope you find the book useful. Thank you, and happy reading!

Connecting to Cisco equipment via the Serial Console

Cisco equipment typically comes without any configuration preloaded on the device. Without a configuration the only method to access the equipment is via the console port which is typically located on the back of the switch or router as shown in the picture below.

To connect to the device you will need to connect a rollover cable from the console port of the Cisco router or switch to the serial port on your computer.

Most modern computers no longer include serial ports. Luckily, USB to Serial adapters are available relatively cheaply. You may need to install the drivers from the manufacturer before the serial adapter can work for you.

Terminal Emulator Configuration

Once you have connected the cable to your computer, you will need a terminal emulator program to log into the device. If you are using Microsoft Windows a popular and free terminal emulator, telnet, and ssh client is called putty. You can download it at http://www.putty.org/. If you are using Apple OS X or Linux, minicom is a common option.

Putty Configuration

Once you have installed the Putty and the drivers for your serial to usb adapter, locate the COM port number of your serial device. To do this open device manager and check under Ports (COM & LPT). In this example I am using COM4.

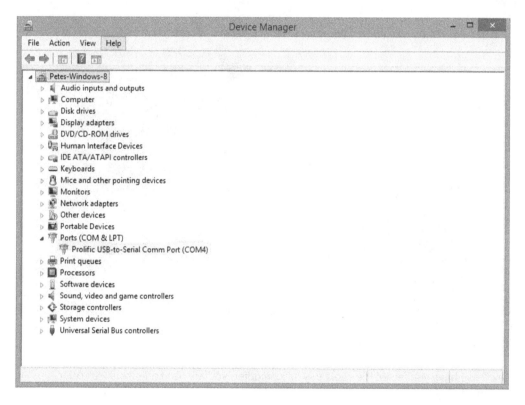

Once you know the COM port number open Putty and verify your serial settings are correct. Check under **Connections > Serial.** The default settings should be correct - 9600 bits per second, 8 data bits, 1 stop bit, no parity, flow control XON/XOFF, as shown below.

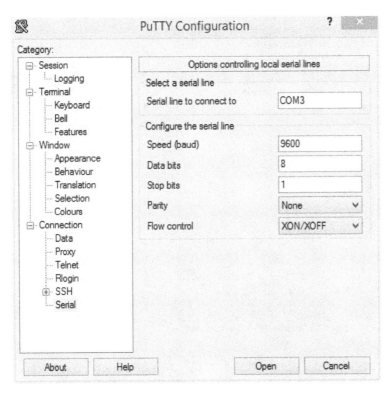

Once you have verified your settings, you can connect using the **Session** tab. Select **Serial** as the **Connection Type** and enter the COM port you are using. In this case, I am using COM3. When you are ready, press Open.

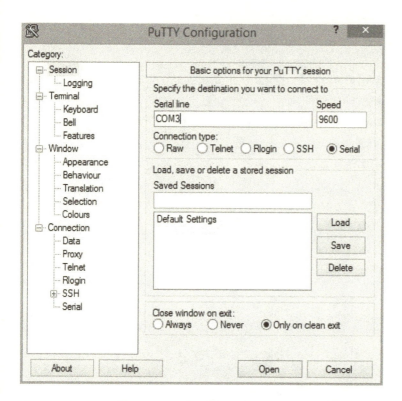

You should see a black terminal window open like in the picture below. Press enter a few times, and if you see something like this you are connected successfully!

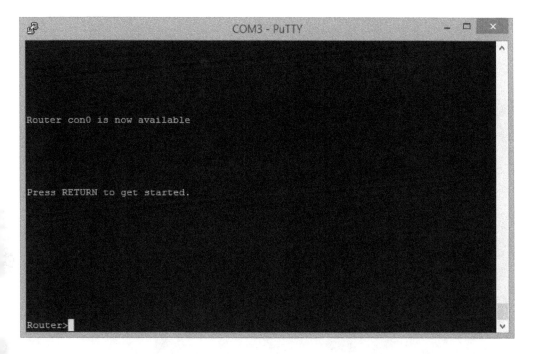

Minicom Configuration

Minicom is a terminal emulator client used on *nix systems such as Linux or Macintosh OS X. Its configuration is similar to that of putty but it is a terminal program, running in the command line interface of the system.

First, install the application. For linux based systems, you can download minicom using the included package manager. For example, in debian based systems you could use

```
$sudo apt-get install minicom
```

For OS X you can download Minicom as well as recieve great instructions at http://pbxbook.com/other/mac-tty.html.

After installing minicom, you must find the tty number which is similar to that of the COM port number on windows. On Linux, you can find this by executing the following command

```
$sudo dmesg | grep tty
```

In the example below example, I see my serial adapter show up as ttyUSB0.

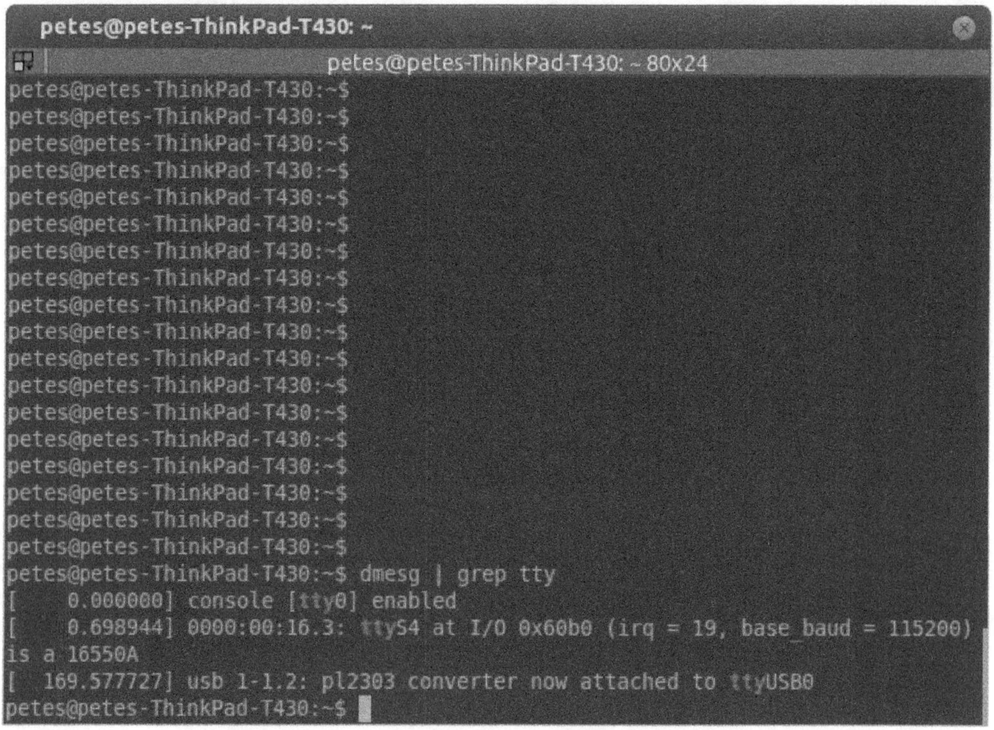

```
petes@petes-ThinkPad-T430: ~
                    petes@petes-ThinkPad-T430: ~ 80x24
petes@petes-ThinkPad-T430:~$
petes@petes-ThinkPad-T430:~$
petes@petes-ThinkPad-T430:~$
petes@petes-ThinkPad-T430:~$
petes@petes-ThinkPad-T430:~$
petes@petes-ThinkPad-T430:~$
petes@petes-ThinkPad-T430:~$
petes@petes-ThinkPad-T430:~$
petes@petes-ThinkPad-T430:~$
petes@petes-ThinkPad-T430:~$
petes@petes-ThinkPad-T430:~$
petes@petes-ThinkPad-T430:~$
petes@petes-ThinkPad-T430:~$
petes@petes-ThinkPad-T430:~$
petes@petes-ThinkPad-T430:~$
petes@petes-ThinkPad-T430:~$
petes@petes-ThinkPad-T430:~$
petes@petes-ThinkPad-T430:~$
petes@petes-ThinkPad-T430:~$ dmesg | grep tty
[    0.000000] console [tty0] enabled
[    0.698944] 0000:00:16.3: ttyS4 at I/O 0x60b0 (irq = 19, base_baud = 115200)
is a 16550A
[  169.577727] usb 1-1.2: pl2303 converter now attached to ttyUSB0
petes@petes-ThinkPad-T430:~$
```

Once you have found the tty, you can configure minicom using the following command.

$sudo minicom -s

Choose serial port setup and configure the correct defaults for cisco routers, namely 9600 bits per second, 8 data bits, 1 stop bit, no parity, flow control XON/XOFF, as shown below. Don't forget to change the serial device to the correct tty. Press exit and select "Save setup as def" to save your settings.

```
petes@petes-ThinkPad-T430: ~

                     petes@petes-ThinkPad-T430: ~ 80x24


    +-----------------------------------------------------------------------+
    | A -     Serial Device      : /dev/ttyUSB0                             |
    | B - Lockfile Location      : /var/lock                                |
    | C -    Callin Program      :                                          |
    | D -   Callout Program      :                                          |
    | E -     Bps/Par/Bits       : 9600 8N1                                 |
    | F - Hardware Flow Control  : Yes                                      |
    | G - Software Flow Control  : No                                       |
    |                                                                       |
    |    Change which setting? █                                            |
    +------------+------------------------------+---------------------------+
                 | Screen and keyboard          |
                 | Save setup as dfl            |
                 | Save setup as..              |
                 | Exit                         |
                 | Exit from Minicom            |
                 +------------------------------+
```

Next, open up the serial connection with

$sudo minicom

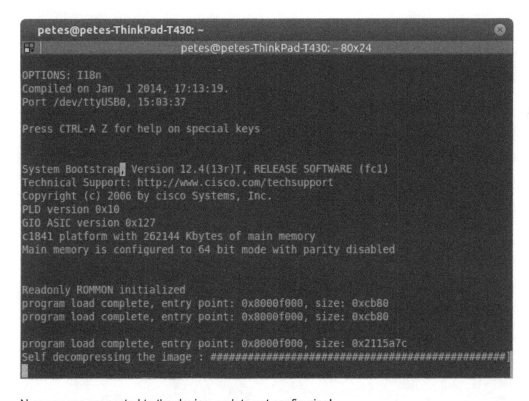

Now you are connected to the device, so lets get configuring!

Initial Configuration Dialog

Upon connecting to a new router or switch you will be greeted with the initial configuration dialog. This dialog helps new users automatically create a basic configuration on the device.

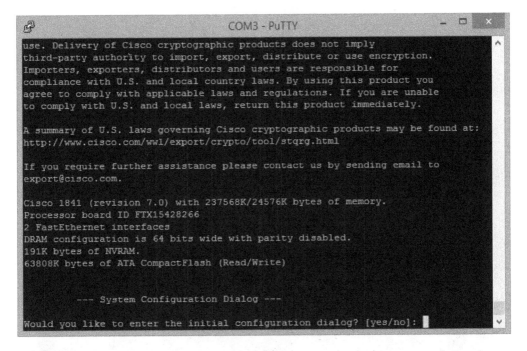

If you'd like to check it out, enter yes and go through the prompted questions. The dialog
prompts you for basic device configuration data, such as setting a host name, password, and IP
address information. I suggest you try the initial configuration dialog out, but I find it is easier to
configure the device manually.

If you would like to manually configure these setting, enter no and you can begin configuring the
device immediately.

Access Levels

Lets take a quick overview of the privilege levels in Cisco IOS. We'll be going into more detail on
which level is used for what in the coming chapters.

When you first connect to a Cisco device, you will see `router>` or `switch>`. The > prompt
means you are in User EXEC mode, the lowest level of privilege to the system.

To enter Privileged EXEC mode on the system, execute the `enable` command. This will grant
administrator access to the device. The prompt will change to `#` illustrating Privileged EXEC
mode.

Once in Privileged Exec mode, you can enter Global Configuration mode using the `Configure Terminal` command. This is where most changes to the system will be made. Notice the prompt change to `(config)#` to illustrate we are now in Global Configuration Mode.

To exit Global Configuration Mode and return to Privileged EXEC mode, use the `exit` command.

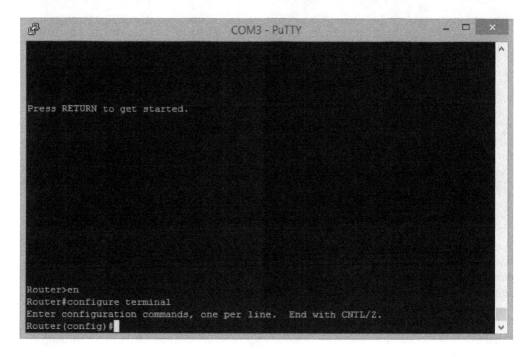

Access level commands overview:

`enable` - Enters Privileged EXEC Mode
`configure terminal` - Enters Global Configuration Mode
`exit` - Exits Global Configuration Mode

Basic Privileged Exec Mode Commands

Privileged Exec mode (the mode indicated by the `#` prompt) is mostly for gathering information about the system. Below are some very helpful commands which can be executed in this mode.

`#copy running-config startup-config`

A commonly used command which writes the current running configuration to NVRAM to be loaded upon next reboot. A shortcut to this lengthy command is #write. You can also choose to write the running config to other locations as well such as an ftp, scp, or tftp server or to a usb flash drive for backup purposes, something we'll cover later.

```
#show running-config
```

This command shows the configuration currently running on the device which is stored in volatile memory. This means the running configuration will be cleared upon reboot unless it has been saved to the startup configuration. You can scroll through the output using the spacebar or by pressing enter on the keyboard.

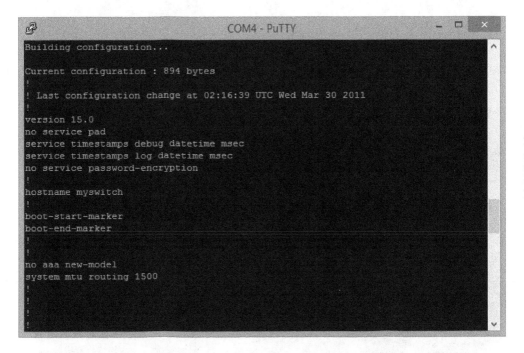

```
#show startup-config
```

This command shows the startup configuration stored in the NVRAM (Flash Memory) of the device. The startup configuration will be loaded to the device upon reboot. Its format is the same as the running-config. Remember that the startup config and running config can be different, if you have modified the configuration since the system has started.

```
#show version
```

This command gives lots of information including the Cisco IOS version number, uptime, amount of system memory, amount of flash memory, model number, number of interfaces, and more.

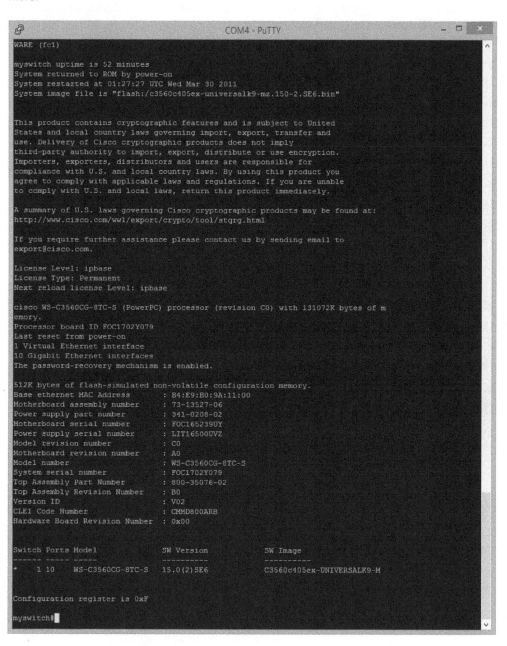

```
WARE (fc1)

myswitch uptime is 52 minutes
System returned to ROM by power-on
System restarted at 01:27:27 UTC Wed Mar 30 2011
System image file is "flash:/c3560c405ex-universalk9-mz.150-2.SE6.bin"


This product contains cryptographic features and is subject to United
States and local country laws governing import, export, transfer and
use. Delivery of Cisco cryptographic products does not imply
third-party authority to import, export, distribute or use encryption.
Importers, exporters, distributors and users are responsible for
compliance with U.S. and local country laws. By using this product you
agree to comply with applicable laws and regulations. If you are unable
to comply with U.S. and local laws, return this product immediately.

A summary of U.S. laws governing Cisco cryptographic products may be found at:
http://www.cisco.com/wwl/export/crypto/tool/stqrg.html

If you require further assistance please contact us by sending email to
export@cisco.com.

License Level: ipbase
License Type: Permanent
Next reload license Level: ipbase

cisco WS-C3560CG-8TC-S (PowerPC) processor (revision C0) with 131072K bytes of m
emory.
Processor board ID FOC1702Y079
Last reset from power-on
1 Virtual Ethernet interface
10 Gigabit Ethernet interfaces
The password-recovery mechanism is enabled.

512K bytes of flash-simulated non-volatile configuration memory.
Base ethernet MAC Address       : B4:E9:B0:9A:11:00
Motherboard assembly number     : 73-13527-06
Power supply part number        : 341-0208-02
Motherboard serial number       : FOC165239UY
Power supply serial number      : LIT16500UVZ
Model revision number           : C0
Motherboard revision number     : A0
Model number                    : WS-C3560CG-8TC-S
System serial number            : FOC1702Y079
Top Assembly Part Number        : 800-35076-02
Top Assembly Revision Number    : B0
Version ID                      : V02
CLEI Code Number                : CMMD800ARB
Hardware Board Revision Number  : 0x00


Switch Ports Model          SW Version        SW Image
------ ----- -----          ----------        ----------
*    1 10    WS-C3560CG-8TC-S  15.0(2)SE6      C3560c405ex-UNIVERSALK9-M


Configuration register is 0xF

myswitch#
```

```
#show inventory
```

This command lists the device descriptions, product IDs, and serial numbers. If the Cisco hardware is modular, the command will also show information about all installed modules.

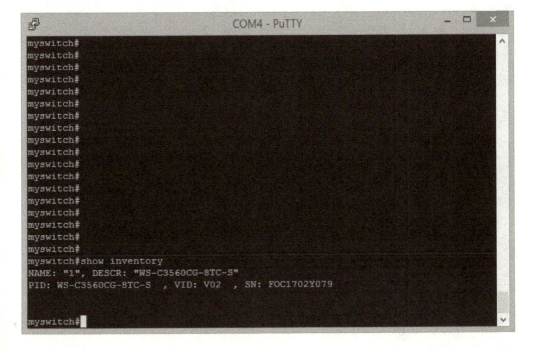

```
#show license all
```

This command lists all of the licenses installed on the device. Notice this information can be found in the `#show version` command as well!

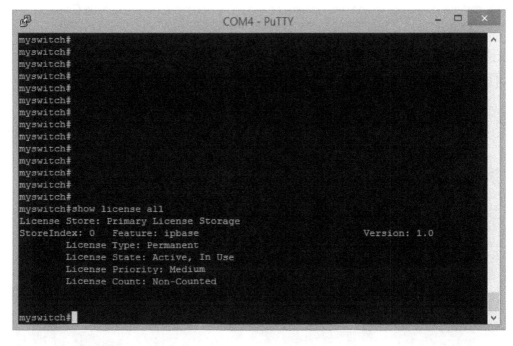

```
#show interfaces
```

This command shows detailed information about the interfaces, such as ip address, MTU, duplex and speed, input and output rate, packets received, and much more.

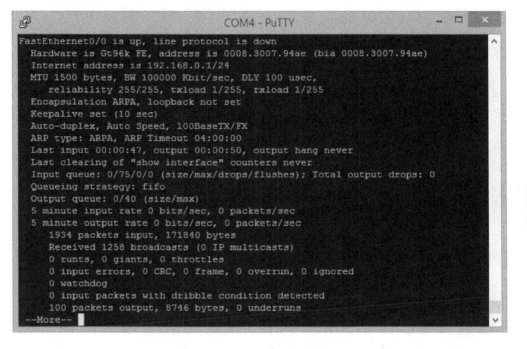

```
#show ip interface brief
```

To get a quick view of the interfaces on the system and their IP address information, execute the #show ip interface brief command. This command also quickly tells you if the interface is up in the "status" and "protocol" fields.

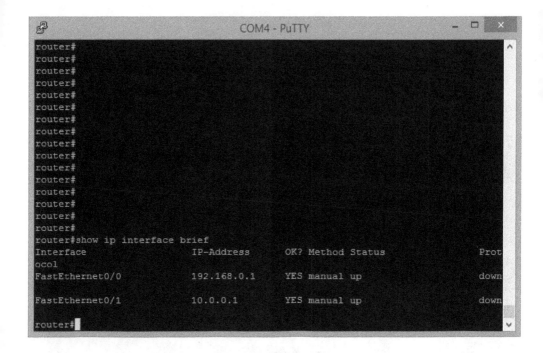

Command Line Interface (CLI) Operators

Shortened Commands

In the Cisco CLI, commands can be shortened by entering only the first few characters of the command, as long as there is no confusion about which command is being entered. For example, typing `"e"` would be insufficient because it could mean either `"enable"` or `"exit"` but typing `"en"` is interpreted as `"enable"` because no other commands start with the characters `e` and `n`. This is very handy to save a few keystrokes!

For educational purposes this book will try to use commands in their full form, but feel free to use the shortened form when testing them out.

Using ?

If you are unsure of the syntax of a certain IOS command, you can use the question mark (?) to give you hints for completing the command. This is very handy for learning all the options of any command. In the example below, I am using the "?" to list the `#show license` sub commands.

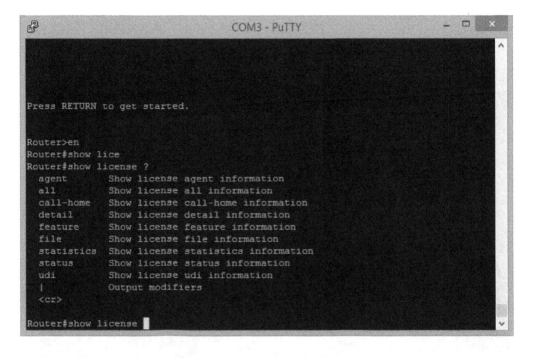

Operators and the Pipe |

The pipe character "|" is used in cisco IOS to search through or filter the output of commands. It allows a user to search through lengthy command outputs to find only the relevant information.

A useful command is the `include` operator. If you are familiar with Linux, Its operation is similar to the use of `grep`. Only lines with the specified data will be output to the screen. For example, if I want to only see lines with the word "interface" in the running configuration, I could run the following command:

```
#show running-config | include interface
```

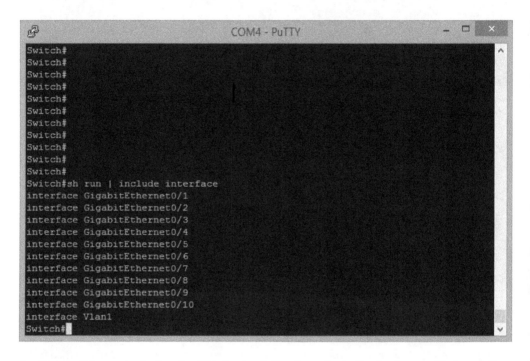

Another useful operator is `begin`. This begins listing the output after the keyword is found. For example, If I only want to see information after the keyword "interface Vlan1" in the running configuration I could use the following command.

```
#show running-config | begin interface Vlan1
```

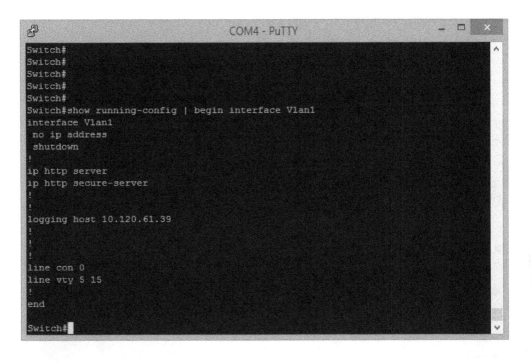

```
Switch#
Switch#
Switch#
Switch#
Switch#
Switch#show running-config | begin interface Vlan1
interface Vlan1
 no ip address
 shutdown
!
ip http server
ip http secure-server
!
!
logging host 10.120.61.39
!
!
!
line con 0
line vty 5 15
!
end

Switch#
```

The Do Command

When you are in Global Configuration Mode, you may execute Privileged Exec commands
using the do command. Without this command, you cannot run privileged exec mode
commands such as show running-config while in global configuration mode. This is useful
as it allows you to execute show commands and writing configurations while actively configuring
the device.

In the example below, I execute the #show clock command while at the interface
configuration prompt. Cool!

```
COM3 - PuTTY                                                    _  □  ×

Press RETURN to get started.










Router>enable
Router#configure terminal
Enter configuration commands, one per line.  End with CNTL/Z.
Router(config)#interface fastethernet 0/0
Router(config-if)#do show clock
*19:46:44.071 UTC Sat Jun 21 2014
Router(config-if)#
```

Chapter 2- Managing Routers and Switches

Remote Administration

Its not always possible to use a console cable to perform changes to Cisco device configurations. What if the Router is at a remote site, or you are working from home? Luckily Cisco allows remote administration using two technologies, Telnet and SSH.

SSH is the prefered method of remote administration because it encrypts data in transit, while telnet does not. By default SSH Version 1 is activated but SSH Version 2 can be enabled manually for increased security.

Telnet

To enable telnet access, you must modify the configuration of the virtual terminal (vty) lines using the `line` command in global configuration mode.

You must specify the virtual terminal lines you would like to modify, in this case we are modifying the first 5 lines, 0-4. That means a total of 5 remote connections can be ongoing at once. Different hardware models can support more than just 5 vty's.

When you are configuring the vty lines, you will notice the prompt has changed to (config-line)# to illustrate you are in the line configuration submode.

Next, specify a telnet password using the `(config-line)#password` command.

By default, the vty lines are disabled. To allow users to connect, the `(config-line)#login` command must be used.

```
(config)#line vty 0 4
(config-line)#password example
(config-line)#login
```

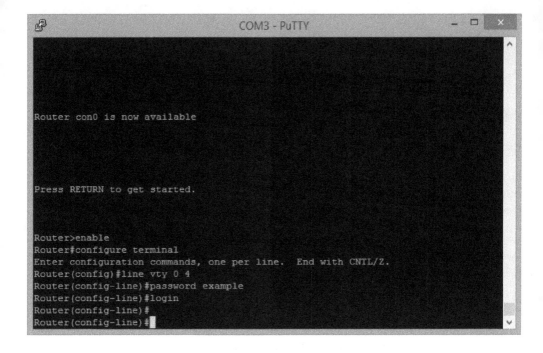

```
                                    COM3 - PuTTY                    _  □  ×

Router con0 is now available




Press RETURN to get started.


Router>enable
Router#configure terminal
Enter configuration commands, one per line.  End with CNTL/Z.
Router(config)#line vty 0 4
Router(config-line)#password example
Router(config-line)#login
Router(config-line)#
Router(config-line)#
```

SSH

To enable logins using the more secure SSH, you must first enable AAA (Authentication, Authorization, and Accounting) and generate an RSA key used for the cryptographic functions of SSH.

To enable AAA globally, execute the `(config)#aaa new-model` command from global configuration mode.

Next, we must generate an RSA key. A domain name is required to generate an RSA key, and can be specified using the `(config)#ip domain name x` command.

To generate the key, use the `(config)#crypto key generate rsa` command. You will be prompted for a key length, choose a key length of at least 768 bits for SSH Version 2. It is also possible to set the key length in the generate command by specifying the modulus using the `(config)#crypto key generate rsa modulus 2048` command. In this example I am using a key length of 2048 bits.

Next, enable SSH Version 2 globally with the following command `(config)#ip ssh version 2`.

We need to create a user to login via SSH using the username command. Simply type `(config)#username x secret x`. Remember, always use secret passwords over unencrypted passwords!

Lastly we must modify the VTY lines to only accept logins via SSH. Enter the vty line configuration using the line command as in the Telnet example. Then specify the login type using `(config-line)# transport input ssh`.

Example:

```
(config)#aaa new-model
(config)#ip domain name example.com
(config)#crypto key generate rsa modulus 2048
(config)#ip ssh version 2
(config)#username x secret x
(config)# line vty 0 4
(config-line)# transport input ssh
```

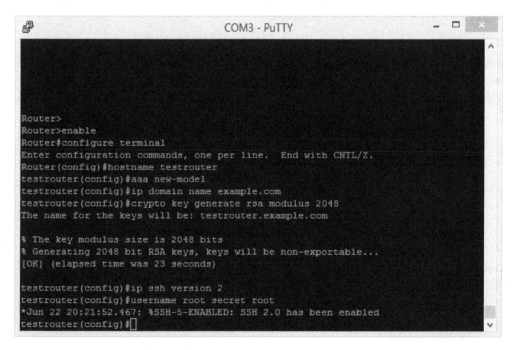

Enabling SCP for secure file copy

There are many occasions when an administrator will need to copy a file to or from a remote Cisco device. When the device is physically present, copying files using a USB flash drive is simple and painless, but that opinion is not always available.

Methods to do so include FTP, TFTP, HTTP, and SCP. However, all but the last method are unencrypted, meaning anyone could spy in on the data being transferred.

To enable the SCP server and to allow encrypted file transfer via the SSH protocol, use the following commands. First you must enable Authentication, Authorization, and Accounting (AAA) globally and create the username and password to be used. Users must be authorized to execute commands (such as scp), and must be given a privilege level of 15 to allow files to be copied. Finally, the SCP server can be enabled.

TIP
It is important to weigh the advantage of this functionality vs its security concerns. Of course you can always just change the privilege level to 15 only when you are SCPing a file, and then change it right back.

```
(config)#aaa new-model
(config)#aaa authentication login default local
(config)#aaa authorization exec default local none
(config)#username root secret xxxxxx
(config)#username root privilege 15
(config)#ip scp server enable
```

If you are using Windows, use a SCP client such as Filezilla or WinSCP to copy files to the Cisco device.

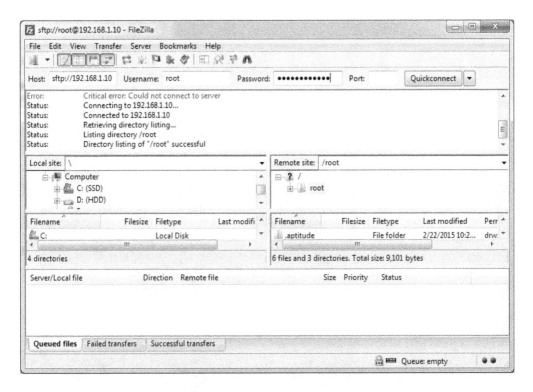

To copy a file from a Linux or OSX computer to a Cisco device using SCP, use the scp command as shown below.

```
$scp ./c1900-universalk9-mz.SPA.151-4.M7.bin root@69.163.56.156:c1900-
universalk9-mz.SPA.151-4.M7.bin
```

This command copies an image file from the local directory on the computer to the root directory of the flash: file system on the remote Cisco device. The username configured on the Cisco device is root, illustrated by root@.

Managing Configurations

Backing Up Configuration Files

Backing up configuration files is a simple process in IOS. Every time you use the `#copy running-config startup-config` command you are writing the configuration to flash memory, NVRAM. If you would like to backup the configuration file elsewhere, simply save the file to another location, such as a USB drive or SCP server.

For example, to backup the configuration to a USB drive, first find the name of the usb drive using the #show file systems command. In this example, the name of the usb drive is usbflash0.

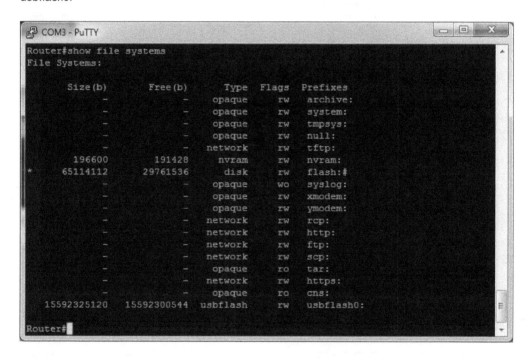

Next, copy to running config to a filename of your choice on the device.

```
#copy running-config usbflash0:backup.txt
```

You can also copy your configuration to a SCP Server using the syntax below.

```
#copy running-config scp://192.168.1.1/
```

```
Router#
Router#
Router#
Router#
Router#
Router#
Router#
Router#
Router#
Router#
Router#
Router#
Router#
Router#copy running-config scp://192.168.1.10
Address or name of remote host [192.168.1.10]?
Destination username [Router]? root
Destination filename [router-confg]?
Writing router-confg
Password:
 Sink: C0644 830 router-confg
!
830 bytes copied in 6.712 secs (124 bytes/sec)

Router#
```

TIP

Some settings are not backed up in configuration files. For example the generation of SSH keys. These types of commands must be added to configuration files manually, or else they must be rerun when the configuration is restored.

Restoring Configuration Files

It is a good idea to write your device configurations on your computer rather than configuring the routers and switches by hand. This allows you to create simple templates that can be modified for the occasion and allows for easy version control and backup through services such as git. If you are unfamiliar with version control, a great place to start learning git is at https://github.com/.

Git allows for a centrally managed, version controlled, secure location for your configuration files. These configs can then be redeployed or adapted at a moment's notice on any failed hardware or new site needs.

A configuration file is simply a list of commands run on the device sequentially. Think of it as a faster way to copy and paste into the terminal window.

To create a configuration file, simply write the commands as you would type them You can see some examples in the appendix section of this book. Test configurations out on lab equipment to create a template you can use for future devices.

To load the configuration file onto the router, copy the configuration file from USB or SCP into the device's running config using the copy command. For example:

```
#copy usbflash1:config.txt running-config
```

or

```
#copy scp://192.168.1.10/config.txt running-config
```

TIP

Cisco configurations are additive - meaning copying a configuration over an existing one may cause conflicts. Its best to reset a router to factory defaults before copying over a new configuration file, to make certain there are no conflicts. We'll go over this process later in this section.

Archive Feature

It is very important to back up configuration files for Cisco devices. This creates a record of what changes have been made and gives a reference to roll back to.

To automatically back up configuration changes to a remote host, use the Archive feature on Cisco IOS. I would recommend using SCP for this procedure to keep your configuration data encrypted in transit. The example below copies the timestamped configuration to the home directory of bob.

```
(config)#archive
(config-archive)#path scp://bob@172.16.1.10/~
```

To archive the current configuration, execute the following command in privileged exec mode:

```
#archive config
```

You can also force archiving configurations upon executing the copy running-config startup-config or write memory commands with the configuration below:

```
(config-archive)#write-memory
```

To check out the recent archives, use the show archive command:

```
#show archive
```

```
COM4 - PuTTY                                                    -  □  ×

Router#
Router#
Router#
Router#
Router#
Router#
Router#
Router#
Router#
Router#show archive
The maximum archive configurations allowed is 10.
The next archive file will be named scp://petes@192.168.1.10/~-<timestamp>-2
 Archive #   Name
     1          scp://petes@192.168.1.10/~-Mar--7-16-47-46.127-0
     2          scp://petes@192.168.1.10/~-Mar--7-16-48-34.147-1 <- Most Recent
     3
     4
     5
     6
     7
     8
     9
    10
Router#[]
```

And you can rollback to a previous configuration as well using the configure replace command.

```
#configure replace scp://172.16.1.10/-Jul--3-17-59-36.018-0
```

Factory Defaults

From the Command Line

If you have privileged exec (enable) access to the router or switch, the easiest way to reset the device to factory default is using the #write erase command.

This command will clear all configuration settings from NVRAM (the startup-config), and upon rebooting the system will return to factory defaults. After clearing the NVRAM, you must reboot the device with the #reset command so the machine can restart with the default configuration. Do not save the running config to NVRAM when prompted, or you will have to restart the process after a lengthy reboot!

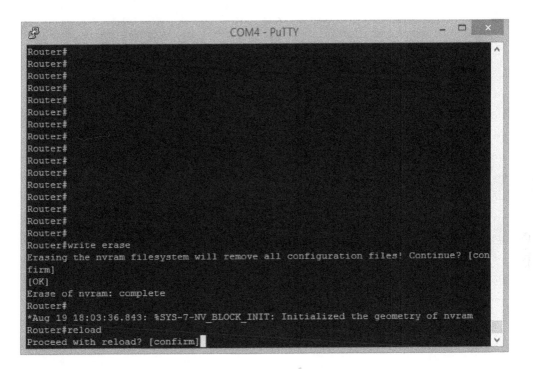

Resetting Switches

If you do not have privileged exec access to the device, (you have forgotten the password, for example) there are still options! Most switches can be reset by holding the Reset button, or in some cases the Mode button. To Reset 3650 Switches for example, press the mode button (pictured below) for 10 seconds.

One minor caveat of Cisco switches is that VLAN data (show vlan) persists after a reset to factory defaults. Why? Because the VLAN information is stored in a separate file in flash memory. If you want to reset the VLAN information as well, you must delete the vlan.dat file in the flash filesystem.

To clear VLAN information, delete the vlan configuration file on flash. The effect will take place after a reboot.

```
#delete flash:/vlan.dat
```

Resetting Routers

Most routers do not have reset buttons. Instead, you can instruct the system to boot factory defaults by changing the configuration register.

The configuration register is responsible for many configuration options on Cisco equipment. It is not often directly configured, as it is capable of manipulating the startup sequence. In this case, that is exactly what we want to do! We can instruct the system to skip loading the startup configuration file stored in flash, loading the default configuration instead.

Modifying the control register can take place from ROM Monitor mode. This is an very basic environment similar to the BIOS on a PC.

To enter ROM Monitor mode press the break key (which is not on all keyboards) from a terminal during device start up.

TIP
If you do not have a break key, putty allows you to enter enter ROM Monitor mode by right clicking on the window and selecting Special Command > Break. In Minicom, the break key is 'Ctrl-A' and then 'F'.

The below commands instruct the system to load a default configuration.

```
a cold start
*Aug 19 17:44:37.163: %SYS-6-BOOTTIME: Time taken to reboot after reload =  103
seconds
Router>
Router>en
Router#reload
Proceed with reload? [confirm]

*Aug 19 17:44:51.327: %SYS-5-RELOAD: Reload requested by console. Reload Reason:
 Reload Command.
System Bootstrap, Version 12.4(13r)T, RELEASE SOFTWARE (fc1)
Technical Support: http://www.cisco.com/techsupport
Copyright (c) 2006 by cisco Systems, Inc.
PLD version 0x10
GIO ASIC version 0x127
c1841 platform with 262144 Kbytes of main memory
Main memory is configured to 64 bit mode with parity disabled


Readonly ROMMON initialized
rommon 1 > confreg 0x2142


You must reset or power cycle for new config to take effect
rommon 2 > reset
```

ROM Monitor Example:

```
rommon 1 > confreg 0x2142
rommon 2 > reset
```

Now you are back into the device! Clear the old configuration with the `#write erase` command and you should be back in business.

Don't forget to change the config register back to default again, so it will subsequently load configuration files from NVRAM. You can do that in IOS using the `(config)#config-register` command.

```
(config)# config-register 0x2102
```

Upgrading Cisco IOS

It is best to have all of your Cisco equipment running the same version of Cisco IOS. This allow you to have a consistent environment with a minimum of conflicts due to incompatible versions and makes it easier to troubleshoot/find any issues caused by IOS bugs.

To upgrade your devices you must first download the IOS image you would like to use from Cisco's website. Login and search for your device under **Support > Downloads.** Once you have found your model, choose **Software on Chassis > IOS Software.**

Often Cisco will show you the recommended or suggested images for your switch or router. This is a good place to start and you can look over the release notes for each image to determine if it will work well in your environment. Once you have chosen your image, download it to proceed.

Once you have the image there are multiple ways to copy it over to your system such as USB, FTP, TFTP, SCP, and HTTP.

If you have physical access to a device with a USB port, the simplest method is to copy it over is from a USB stick which is formatted with the FAT32 file system. Simply copy your IOS image onto the flash drive and plug it into the USB port of the router or switch.

When you plug the USB stick into the router or switch, it will show up as device `usb0:` or `usbflash0:` or similar. You can check the path to your USB stick using the `#show file systems` command. In the example below, the usb stick shows up as `usbflash0:`

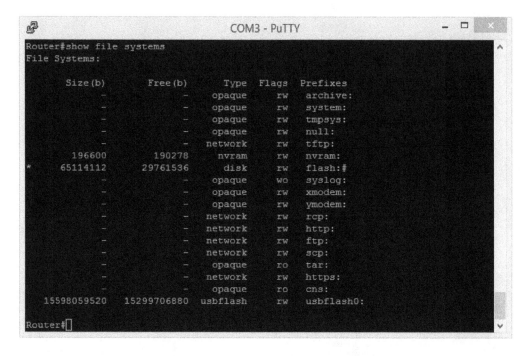

```
                                  COM3 - PuTTY                            _  □  ×
Router#show file systems
File Systems:

        Size(b)        Free(b)       Type   Flags   Prefixes
              -              -      opaque     rw    archive:
              -              -      opaque     rw    system:
              -              -      opaque     rw    tmpsys:
              -              -      opaque     rw    null:
              -              -     network     rw    tftp:
         196600         190278       nvram     rw    nvram:
*      65114112       29761536        disk     rw    flash:#
              -              -      opaque     wo    syslog:
              -              -      opaque     rw    xmodem:
              -              -      opaque     rw    ymodem:
              -              -     network     rw    rcp:
              -              -     network     rw    http:
              -              -     network     rw    ftp:
              -              -     network     rw    scp:
              -              -      opaque     ro    tar:
              -              -     network     rw    https:
              -              -      opaque     ro    cns:
    15598059520    15299706880    usbflash     rw    usbflash0:

Router#
```

Once the USB stick is inserted, simply copy the IOS image from the flash drive to the local flash memory on the router or switch. You can use the copy command to do so.

For example:
```
#copy usbflash0:c1841-ipbasek9-mz.151-4.M.bin flash:
```

This command will copy the image stored on the usb drive to the onboard flash memory of the router.

You can also experiment with copying from other sources, such as FTP, TFTP, HTTP, HTTPS, and SCP servers.

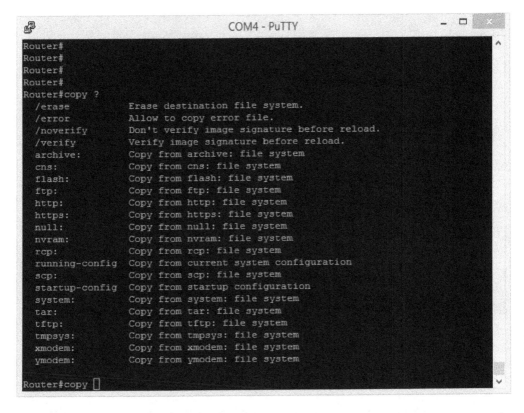

Many administrators choose to use TFTP to transfer images and configuration files because of its easy setup. But remember - TFTP is unencrypted and should not be used over the public internet!

To transfer files via TFTP, use the copy command specifying TFTP as the source. You will be prompted for the TFTP server address, source (remote) filename, and destination (local) filename.

For Example:

(config)#copy tftp flash

```
COM4 - PuTTY                                            -  □  ×
Router#
Router#
Router#
Router#
Router#
Router#
Router#
Router#
Router#
Router#
Router#
Router#
Router#
Router#
Router#
Router#
Router#
Router#
Router#
Router#copy tftp flash
Address or name of remote host []? 192.168.1.1
Source filename []? iosimage
Destination filename [iosimage]?
Accessing tftp://192.168.1.1/iosimage...
```

Once the copy is complete, you can choose the IOS image to load on next boot using the `boot system` command. Its a good idea to issue the `no boot system` command first, to clear the current boot settings.

These commands instruct the system to load the specified IOS image on next reboot.

```
(config)#no boot system
(config)#boot system flash:1841-ipbasek9-mz.151-4.M.bin
```

TIP

The boot setting is stored in the configuration file. If you clear the configuration Cisco devices default to boot IOS images in alphabetical order - that usually means the oldest image first, assuming you have not changed the name of the images.

Because of this, you may prefer to delete the older image from flash, keeping only the newer image. Only do this once you have verified everything is working as expected!

Chapter 3 - Advanced Configurations

Dynamic Host Configuration Protocol (DHCP)

DHCP is used by client computers to automatically receive an IP address on the network. Multiple DHCP servers are available, such as Microsoft DHCP Server on Windows, or dhcpd on Linux. Cisco also provides a DHCP server in IOS which is fairly straightforward to configure, and does not require the configuration/maintenance of any external DHCP server.

The DHCP server is configured per subnet and requires a physical or Vlan interface to be present on the subnet to function.

Basic DHCP Configuration

To configure the DHCP server, you must specify a DHCP pool name, the network address, a default search domain to be given to clients, a DNS server, and a default gateway. All this is done in the DHCP configuration mode. See the simple example below:

```
(config)# ip dhcp pool mypool
(dhcp-config)# network 192.168.1.0
(dhcp-config)# domain-name mydomain.com
(dhcp-config)# dns-server 8.8.8.8 8.8.4.4
(dhcp-config)# default-router 192.168.1.1
```

TIP
The cisco device has to have an interface on the configured network, in this case the 192.168.1.0 network, to assign DHCP leases in the pool. For example, hosts connected to gi0/0 configured with ip 192.168.1.1 will recive addresses from the pool above.

```
COM4 - PuTTY                                                    — □ X

Switch#
Switch#
Switch#
Switch#
Switch#
Switch#
Switch#
Switch#
Switch#
Switch#
Switch#
Switch#
Switch#
Switch#
Switch#
Switch#config t
Enter configuration commands, one per line.  End with CNTL/Z.
Switch(config)#ip dhcp pool mypool
Switch(dhcp-config)#network 192.168.1.0
Switch(dhcp-config)#domain-name mydomain.com
Switch(dhcp-config)#dns-server 8.8.8.8 8.8.4.4
Switch(dhcp-config)#default-router 192.168.1.1
Switch(dhcp-config)#exit
Switch(config)#
```

DHCP Options

DHCP options pass optional configuration information onto clients. Example uses of DHCP options include specifying a PXE boot server, time server, or log server to be used by the client. There are a large number of DHCP options which can be configured, which ones you require, if any, depends strongly on your environment.

DHCP Options can be configured using the `(dhcp-config)#option` *option_number* command inside of the corresponding DHCP pool. The example below configures a PXE boot server and image name.

```
(dhcp-config)# option 66 ip 10.0.0.2
(dhcp-config)# option 67 ascii pxelinux.0
```

DHCP Reservations

To reserve certain addresses for static assignment use the excluded-address command in global configuration mode.

```
(config)# ip dhcp excluded-address 192.168.1.1 192.168.1.100
```

The above command prevents the DHCP server from assigning addresses 192.168.1.1-192.168.1.100 to clients.

```
Switch>
Switch>
Switch>
Switch>
Switch>
Switch>
Switch>
Switch>
Switch>
Switch>
Switch>
Switch>
Switch>
Switch>
Switch>
Switch>
Switch>
Switch>en
Switch#config t
Enter configuration commands, one per line.  End with CNTL/Z.
Switch(config)#ip dhcp excluded-address 192.168.1.1 192.168.1.100
Switch(config)#exit
Switch#
```

Static DHCP Assignments

It is also possible to create a static DHCP binding or reservation based on client mac address. Creating a static binding requires making a DHCP pool for the specific client, assigning the client a specific IP address, and specifying the MAC address of the client.

```
(config)#ip dhcp pool Static01
(dhcp-config)#host 192.168.1.10 255.255.255.0
(dhcp-config)#client-identifier 0124.dbad.008a.dd
(dhcp-config)#default-router 192.168.1.1
(dhcp-config)#dns-server 8.8.8.8 8.8.4.4
(dhcp-config)#domain-name mydomain.com
```

The client-identifier is the MAC address of the client computer starting with 01, which denotes the Ethernet media type.

```
COM4 - PuTTY                                                              _  □  X
Switch(config)#
Switch(config)#
Switch(config)#
Switch(config)#
Switch(config)#
Switch(config)#
Switch(config)#
Switch(config)#
Switch(config)#
Switch(config)#
Switch(config)#
Switch(config)#
Switch(config)#
Switch(config)#
Switch(config)#
Switch(config)#ip dhcp pool Static01
Switch(dhcp-config)#host 192.168.1.10 255.255.255.0
Switch(dhcp-config)#client-identifier 0124.dbad.008a.dd
Switch(dhcp-config)#default-router 192.168.1.1
Switch(dhcp-config)#dns-server 8.8.8.8 8.8.4.4
Switch(dhcp-config)#domain-name mydomain.com
Switch(dhcp-config)#exit
Switch(config)#
```

DHCP Forwarding

To pass DHCP broadcasts to an upstream DHCP server, the DHCP forwarding agent can be configured on an interface. Its configuration is very straightforward, simply specify the ip address of the upstream DHCP server using the `(config-if)# ip helper-address x.x.x.x` command.

```
(config)# int vlan 500
(config-if)# ip helper-address 10.0.0.1
```

DHCP Snooping

DHCP Snooping prevents unauthorized DHCP servers from handing out leases to clients. It is configured on a per VLAN basis.

For example, if a client computer or server on a VLAN is running a DHCP server in addition to the DHCP server on your Cisco router or switch, clients may inadvertently receive their IP address from the unauthorized DHCP server. These unauthorised servers could cause the clients to have incorrect or overlapping IP addresses or serve as agents for man in the middle attacks.

To prevent any unauthorised DHCP servers from assigning IP address leases, DHCP snooping can be configured.

```
(config)#ip dhcp snooping
(config)#ip dhcp snooping vlan x,y
```

The first command enables the DHCP snooping feature globally and the second enables the feature on a per VLAN basis. By default, DHCP snooping is disabled on all vlans.

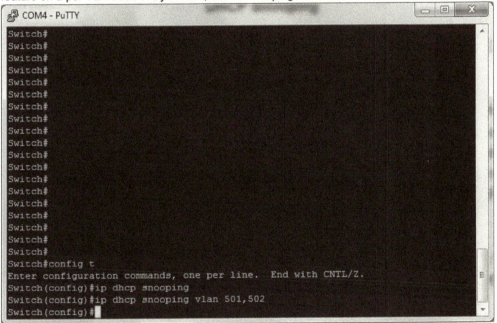

To use this feature with an external DHCP server, the port connected to the DHCP server must be placed in the trusted state.

```
(config-if)# ip dhcp snooping trust
```

To check the status of DHCP snooping, use the following command:

```
#show ip dhcp snooping
```

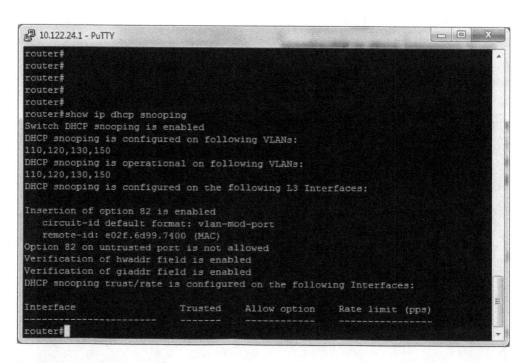

```
10.122.24.1 - PuTTY                                              — ☐ X
router#
router#
router#
router#
router#
router#show ip dhcp snooping
Switch DHCP snooping is enabled
DHCP snooping is configured on following VLANs:
110,120,130,150
DHCP snooping is operational on following VLANs:
110,120,130,150
DHCP snooping is configured on the following L3 Interfaces:

Insertion of option 82 is enabled
   circuit-id default format: vlan-mod-port
   remote-id: e02f.6d99.7400 (MAC)
Option 82 on untrusted port is not allowed
Verification of hwaddr field is enabled
Verification of giaddr field is enabled
DHCP snooping trust/rate is configured on the following Interfaces:

Interface                 Trusted    Allow option    Rate limit (pps)
------------------------  -------    ------------    ----------------
router#
```

Verifying DHCP

Sometimes when troubleshooting it is necessary to find which port a computer is plugged into on a switch. One method to determine this is to search through the mac address table on the switch for the mac address of the machine. You can view the table using the following command:

```
#show mac address-table
```

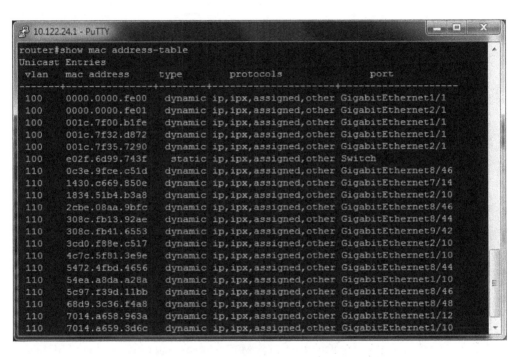

```
10.122.24.1 - PuTTY
router#show mac address-table
Unicast Entries
 vlan   mac address     type      protocols               port
-------+---------------+--------+---------------------+-------------------
 100    0000.0000.fe00   dynamic  ip,ipx,assigned,other  GigabitEthernet1/1
 100    0000.0000.fe01   dynamic  ip,ipx,assigned,other  GigabitEthernet2/1
 100    001c.7f00.b1fe   dynamic  ip,ipx,assigned,other  GigabitEthernet1/1
 100    001c.7f32.d872   dynamic  ip,ipx,assigned,other  GigabitEthernet1/1
 100    001c.7f35.7290   dynamic  ip,ipx,assigned,other  GigabitEthernet2/1
 100    e02f.6d99.743f   static   ip,ipx,assigned,other  Switch
 110    0c3e.9fce.c51d   dynamic  ip,ipx,assigned,other  GigabitEthernet8/46
 110    1430.c669.850e   dynamic  ip,ipx,assigned,other  GigabitEthernet7/14
 110    1834.51b4.b3a8   dynamic  ip,ipx,assigned,other  GigabitEthernet2/10
 110    2cbe.08aa.9bfc   dynamic  ip,ipx,assigned,other  GigabitEthernet8/46
 110    308c.fb13.92ae   dynamic  ip,ipx,assigned,other  GigabitEthernet8/44
 110    308c.fb41.6553   dynamic  ip,ipx,assigned,other  GigabitEthernet9/42
 110    3cd0.f88e.c517   dynamic  ip,ipx,assigned,other  GigabitEthernet2/10
 110    4c7c.5f81.3e9e   dynamic  ip,ipx,assigned,other  GigabitEthernet1/10
 110    5472.4fbd.4656   dynamic  ip,ipx,assigned,other  GigabitEthernet8/44
 110    54ea.a8da.a28a   dynamic  ip,ipx,assigned,other  GigabitEthernet1/10
 110    5c97.f39d.11bb   dynamic  ip,ipx,assigned,other  GigabitEthernet8/46
 110    68d9.3c36.f4a8   dynamic  ip,ipx,assigned,other  GigabitEthernet8/48
 110    7014.a658.963a   dynamic  ip,ipx,assigned,other  GigabitEthernet1/12
 110    7014.a659.3d6c   dynamic  ip,ipx,assigned,other  GigabitEthernet1/10
```

In the example below, I am searching for a specific mac address.

```
#show mac-address table | include 308c.fb41.6553
```

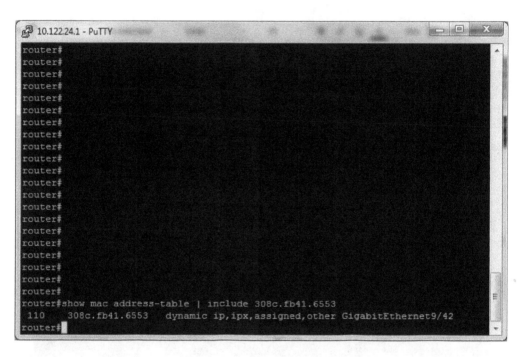

To find the IP address of a computer based on its MAC address, you can search the ARP table. In the example below, I am searching the ARP table for a specific mac address to find the associated IP address.

```
#show ip arp | include 308c.fb41.6553
```

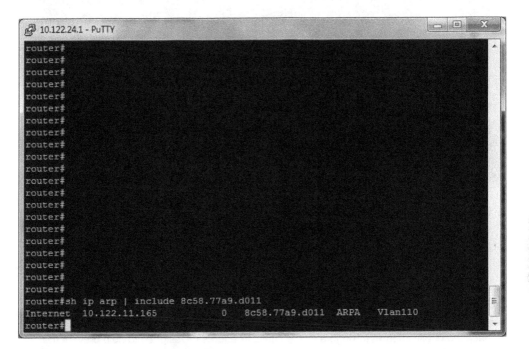

To list the all of the addresses assigned by the Cisco DHCP server you can use the following command:

```
#show ip dhcp binding
```

```
10.122.24.1 - PuTTY

Bindings from all pools not associated with VRF:
IP address          Client-ID/              Lease expiration        Type
                    Hardware address/
                    User name
10.122.10.96        01d8.d1cb.581c.28       Mar 06 2015 06:26 AM    Automatic
10.122.10.131       01ec.3586.376d.08       Mar 06 2015 09:26 AM    Automatic
10.122.10.231       01d8.d1cb.5c77.db       Mar 05 2015 08:04 PM    Automatic
10.122.10.240       01ec.3586.30a4.5a       Mar 06 2015 10:21 AM    Automatic
10.122.10.245       24a2.e165.588f          Infinite                Automatic
10.122.11.42        018c.2daa.3974.6d       Mar 06 2015 09:26 AM    Automatic
10.122.11.63        0124.e314.d7a4.a9       Mar 06 2015 09:13 AM    Automatic
10.122.11.69        019c.04eb.3795.b9       Mar 05 2015 10:20 PM    Automatic
10.122.11.70        018c.2937.1ea1.ef       Mar 06 2015 08:58 AM    Automatic
10.122.11.71        0154.724f.bd46.56       Mar 06 2015 08:38 AM    Automatic
10.122.11.72        0118.2a7b.775f.95       Mar 06 2015 11:28 AM    Automatic
10.122.11.73        0178.fd94.2b5e.a4       Mar 05 2015 06:09 PM    Automatic
10.122.11.74        1430.c669.850e          Mar 06 2015 09:03 AM    Automatic
10.122.11.75        0178.fd94.1a2b.90       Mar 06 2015 09:46 AM    Automatic
10.122.11.76        01f0.2475.7bac.81       Mar 06 2015 11:09 AM    Automatic
10.122.11.79        0154.eaa8.daa2.8a       Mar 06 2015 11:09 AM    Automatic
10.122.11.80        01f8.2793.4950.8a       Mar 06 2015 08:44 AM    Automatic
10.122.11.82        0170.3eac.4c44.78       Mar 06 2015 08:48 AM    Automatic
10.122.11.84        0170.3eac.9628.f0       Mar 06 2015 11:51 AM    Automatic
--More--
```

To clear all DHCP bindings from the system, you can use the following command:

```
#clear ip dhcp binding *
```

Network Address Translation (NAT)

Network Address Translation is typically used to allow multiple computers on a private network to reach the public internet through a single public IP address. Designed to help prevent the exhaustion of IPv4 addresses, NAT allows a site with hundreds of users to only require a single public IP address.

If your router will be providing internet access for many clients it almost certainly will need to be running NAT!

There are a few steps to configuring NAT on a Cisco router. You must specify which interface(s) will be internal (facing the clients) and which will be external (facing the public internet). This is performed with the `ip nat inside/outside` commands.

```
(config)#interface GigabitEthernet0/1
(config-if)#no shutdown
(config-if)#ip address 10.0.0.1 255.255.255.0
(config-if)#ip nat inside
```

```
(config)#interface GigabitEthernet0/0
(config-if)#no shutdown
(config-if)#ip address 50.74.120.91 255.255.255.248
(config-if)#ip nat outside
```

Second, you must create a "NAT pool" specifying the public IP addresses to be used. In this case, the pool's name is "test" and the external address 50.74.120.91 will be used for NATing. The Prefix statement is the subnet mask of the external interface, in this case 255.255.255.248 or /29.

```
(config)# ip nat pool test 50.74.120.91 50.74.120.91 prefix 29
```

Last, an ACL must be created to permit NAT to/from these addresses. We'll cover these in more detail in the security section of this book. The commands below create an access list and assign the ACL to NAT pool "test". This permits clients on the 10.0.0.0/24 network to be NATed. The overload variable means we are performing Port Address Translation, or PNAT, meaning we are using a single Public IP for multiple client computers. Other NAT modes exist, such as one to one NAT, but PNAT is the most common.

```
(config)# access-list 1 permit 10.0.0.0 0.0.0.255
(config)# ip nat inside source list 1 pool test overload
```

Discovery Protocols, CDP and LLDP

Discovery protocols help Network Administrators know what devices are on their network. They list the directly connected neighbors to the device, allowing Administrators to create a working map of the network.

There are two major discovery protocols, Cisco Discovery Protocol (CDP) and Link Layer Discovery Protocol (LLDP). CDP is a cisco proprietary discovery protocol which is enabled by default on most cisco equipment. LLDP is very similar to CDP but is an open standard and can thus be run on equipment from multiple vendors.

CDP

CDP is enabled by default on most cisco equipment. To see information about all the devices running CDP connected to a device, use the following command:

```
#sh cdp neighbors
```

```
router#show cdp neighbors
Capability Codes: R - Router, T - Trans Bridge, B - Source Route Bridge
                  S - Switch, H - Host, I - IGMP, r - Repeater, P - Phone,
                  D - Remote, C - CVTA, M - Two-port Mac Relay

Device ID         Local Intrfce    Holdtme    Capability   Platform   Port ID
08cc68481f8d      Gig 4/29         147            S I      SF302-08P  gi1
SEP0004f2f069f8   Gig 8/19         146            H P      IP Phone   port 1
SEP0004f2ebba16   Gig 8/40         143            H P      IP Phone   port 1
1204123732-router2
                  Gig 2/5          169          R S I      3725       Fas 0/1
1204123732-router1
                  Gig 1/5          177          R S I      3725       Fas 0/1
SEP0004f2eef52a   Gig 7/3          172            H P      IP Phone   port 1
SEP0021D8B9EB4A   Gig 2/42         174          H P M      IP Phone   Port 1
SEP3037A6173B5D   Gig 1/48         160          H P M      IP Phone   Port 1
SEP3037A6173AE6   Gig 7/47         153          H P M      IP Phone   Port 1
SEP001C581C90C0   Gig 9/6          164          H P M      IP Phone   Port 1
SEP001D4560BABD   Gig 2/28         133          H P M      IP Phone   Port 1
SEP001E7AC3CFCC   Gig 2/22         134          H P M      IP Phone   Port 1
SEP00175AEBFACF   Gig 2/24         152            H P      IP Phone   Port 1
SEP0019552CB8C4   Gig 1/19         151          H P M      IP Phone   Port 1
SEP0019305E09CE   Gig 9/2          151          H P M      IP Phone   Port 1
 --More--
```

CDP shows the type of device through the capability tab. For example, two 3725's (which can act as Routers, Switches, and can run IGMP) are connected via gi 2/5 and gi 1/5, through their respective Fa 0/0 interfaces.

LLDP

If you are in a mixed vendor environment LLDP is a great alternative to CDP. To enable LLDP on your Cisco device use the following command:

```
(config)# lldp run
```

Viewing LLDP neighbors is very similar to CDP:

```
#sh lldp neighbors
```

In this example we have a switch (B) directly connected on interface gi 0/8.

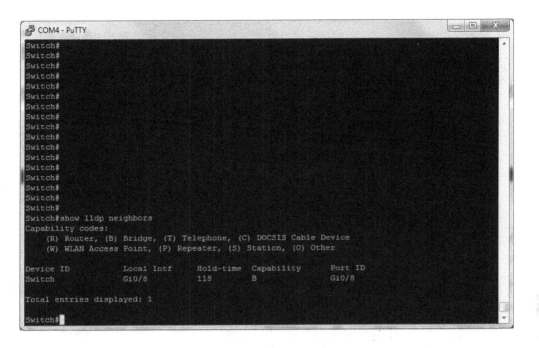

```
Switch#
Switch#
Switch#
Switch#
Switch#
Switch#
Switch#
Switch#
Switch#
Switch#
Switch#
Switch#
Switch#
Switch#
Switch#
Switch#
Switch#show lldp neighbors
Capability codes:
    (R) Router, (B) Bridge, (T) Telephone, (C) DOCSIS Cable Device
    (W) WLAN Access Point, (P) Repeater, (S) Station, (O) Other

Device ID          Local Intf     Hold-time  Capability     Port ID
Switch             Gi0/8          118        B              Gi0/8

Total entries displayed: 1

Switch#
```

High Availability

Network Engineers often have a requirement to build fault tolerant networks. These networks fail over gracefully in the case of a hardware or ISP failure. Otherwise a single failure could down an entire office or data center, affecting hundreds of users!

Two major protocols for establishing high availability gateways are HSRP (Hot Standby Router Protocol) and VRRP (Virtual Router Redundancy Protocol).

HSRP is a cisco proprietary protocol and VRRP is an open standard. Besides this difference they are configured and operate very similarly.

HSRP and VRRP work by creating virtual IP addresses (VIPs). These virtual IP addresses are shared by two or more routers, with the active router using the VIP as its IP address.

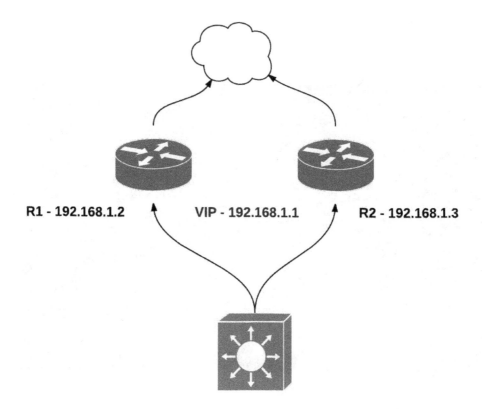

R1 - 192.168.1.2   **VIP - 192.168.1.1**   **R2 - 192.168.1.3**

In the example above, R1 and R2 have addresses 192.168.1.2 and 192.168.1.3 respectively. Together they share the Virtual IP address 192.168.1.1, although only the member with the highest priority will be actively using this address.

In case of a failure of the first router, the second will take over the VIP - and the clients behind it will be none the wiser!

Both HSRP and VRRP are simple to configure. Lets take a look:

HSRP

To configure HSRP enter the interface configurations of the routers and enter the standby IP (the VIP), the priority (higher priorities will be active - the default is 100), and enable preemption. If preemption is enabled, the router with the highest priority becomes the active router. The configuration on the second router is the same, but with a lower priority (the default - 100).

```
R1(config)# interface Gi 0/1
R1(config-if)# ip address 192.168.1.2 255.255.255.0
R1(config-if)# standby 1 ip 192.168.1.1
R1(config-if)# standby 1 priority 200
R1(config-if)# standby 1 preempt

R2(config)# interface Gi 0/1
R2(config-if)# ip address 192.168.1.3 255.255.255.0
R2(config-if)# standby 1 ip 192.168.1.1
R2(config-if)# standby 1 preempt
```

VRRP

The configuration for VRRP is very similar. Instead of standby, use the keyword vrrp. Also, preemption is enabled by default so it is not required to add to the configuration.

```
R1(config)# interface Gi 0/1
R1(config-if)# ip address 192.168.1.2 255.255.255.0
R1(config-if)# vrrp 1 ip 192.168.1.1
R1(config-if)# vrrp 1 priority 110

R2(config)# interface Gig 0/1
R2(config-if)# ip address 192.168.1.3 255.255.255.0
R2(config-if)# vrrp 1 ip 192.168.1.1
```

Chapter 4 - Switching

Modern switches are extremely robust with layer 3 models performing functions originally reserved for routers such as running routing protocols. They are used from the access layer to the core of the network, and in some designs even on the edge. You will certainly be configuring many switches and should have a very strong knowledge of their basics.

Creating/Verifying Vlans

Managed switches are capable of creating multiple Virtual LANs or VLANS on a single physical switch. This allows for Layer 2 separation between different ports on the same switch, logically similar to multiple physical switches.

Between multiple VLANs, the only way to have these separate subnets communicate is through the use of a Layer 3 device performing routing. The Layer 3 switch itself could serve this function, as we'll see later!

To assign ports to different vlans, the VLAN must first be created. To create a vlan, use the `(config)# vlan` command to enter VLAN configuration mode. Specify a vlan number between 1 and 4094. In general it is best to use vlans 1-1001 due to limitations with extended vlans, although VLAN 1006-4094 are available if needed.

If you were wondering, vlans 1002-1005 are reserved for bridging legacy L2 technologies to Ethernet, such as token ring and fddi, and cannot be configured or disabled by users.

To create a vlan, simply enter `(config)# vlan vlan_number`. The name command assigns a name to the vlan, much like the "description" command for interfaces.

```
(config)# vlan 501
(config-vlan)# name "User Network"
```

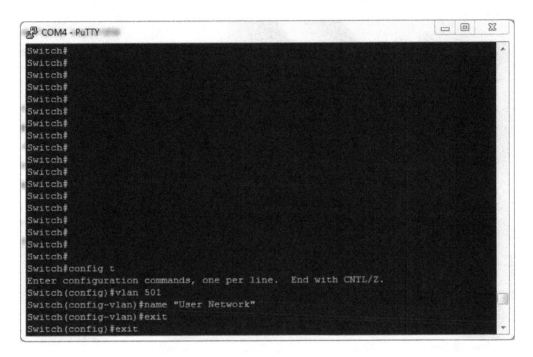

To verify the vlans configured on the device, use the `#show vlan` command.

```
#show vlan
```

```
COM4 - PuTTY                                                        _ □ X

Switch#show vlan

VLAN Name                             Status      Ports
---- --------------------------------  ---------  -------------------------------
1    default                          active      Gi1/0/1, Gi1/0/2, Gi1/0/3
                                                   Gi1/0/4, Gi1/0/5, Gi1/0/6
                                                   Gi1/0/7, Gi1/0/8, Gi1/0/9
                                                   Gi1/0/10, Gi1/0/11, Gi1/0/12
                                                   Gi1/0/13, Gi1/0/14, Gi1/0/15
                                                   Gi1/0/16, Gi1/0/17, Gi1/0/18
                                                   Gi1/0/19, Gi1/0/20, Gi1/0/21
                                                   Gi1/0/22, Gi1/0/23, Gi1/0/24
501  User Network                     active
1002 fddi-default                     act/unsup
1003 token-ring-default               act/unsup
1004 fddinet-default                  act/unsup
1005 trnet-default                    act/unsup

VLAN Type  SAID       MTU    Parent RingNo BridgeNo Stp  BrdgMode Trans1 Trans2
---- ----- ---------- -----  ------ ------ -------- ---- -------- ------ ------
1    enet  100001     1500   -      -      -        -    -        0      0
501  enet  100501     1500   -      -      -        -    -        0      0
1002 fddi  101002     1500   -      -      -        -    -        0      0
1003 tr    101003     1500   -      -      -        -    -        0      0
```

The output of the #show vlan command lists the vlan numbers, names, and ports assigned to each vlan.

Configuring Switch Ports

To configure switch ports, enter interface configuration mode via the global configuration mode command (config)# interface *port_type port_number*

Examples of port types are FastEthernet, GigabitEthernet, and Serial.

The port number is usually represented by two or three numbers separated by forward slashes. For example gigabitEthernet 0/1 or gigabitEthernet 1/0/1. Typically the first number is the switch number, the second is the module number on that switch, and the last is the port number on that module. This varies on different hardware platforms.

To modify the configuration of the first port on a 3750X-24P Switch, execute the following commands:

```
Switch(config)#interface gigabitEthernet 1/0/1
Switch(config-if)#description "User Port"
Switch(config-if)#switchport access vlan 501
Switch(config-if)#switchport mode access
```

```
COM4 - PuTTY                                                  [ - ] [ □ ] [ X ]
Switch#
Switch#
Switch#
Switch#
Switch#
Switch#
Switch#
Switch#
Switch#
Switch#
Switch#
Switch#
Switch#config t
Enter configuration commands, one per line.  End with CNTL/Z.
Switch(config)#interface gi 1/0/1
Switch(config-if)#des
Switch(config-if)#description "User Port"
Switch(config-if)#switchport access vlan 501
Switch(config-if)#switchport mode access
Switch(config-if)#exit
Switch(config)#exit
Switch#
Mar 30 01:37:52.356: %SYS-5-CONFIG_I: Configured from console by console
```

`Switchport access vlan 501` assigns the port to vlan 501, and `switchport mode access` designates the port as an access, or user facing, port - which is the default setting.

Multiple interfaces can likewise be configured simultaneously using the interface range command, this case ports 1-24 on switch 1.

```
Switch(config)#interface range gigabitEthernet 1/0/1-24
Switch(config-if)#description "User Port"
Switch(config-if)#switchport access vlan 501
Switch(config-if)#switchport mode access
```

Configuring Routed Interfaces

Sometimes its necessary to turn a port on a switch to a layer 3 routing interface. This allows the interface to be assigned an IP address directly, behaving just like an interface on a router. SImply specify the `(config-if)#no switchport` command on the interface to enable this mode.

```
Switch(config)#interface GigabitEthernet1/0/2
Switch(config-if)#description "Routed Port"
Switch(config-if)#no switchport
```

```
Switch(config-if)#ip address 10.10.10.10 255.255.255.0
```

Configuring Switch Vlan Interfaces (SVIs)

It is possible to create a layer 3 interface on a vlan. This interface can be used for management, for running a DHCP server, or for serving as a default gateway for a subnet. This type of virtual interface is called a Switch VLAN interface or SVI. It is configured very similarly to a physical interface. This IP address can be reached from any port on the associated VLAN.

TIP
Traffic between SVIs is routed by default if ip routing is enabled - meaning two VLANs with SVIs can communicate, even if that was not intended! This can be resolved via ACLs, as covered in the security section of this book.

```
Switch(config)#interface Vlan501
Switch(config-if)#description "User SVI"
Switch(config-if)#ip address 10.127.0.1 255.255.255.128
```

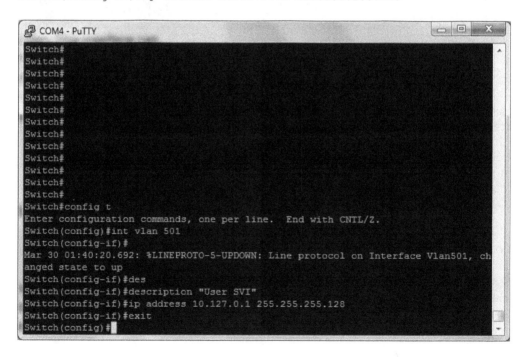

Notice from the `#show interface vlan 501` command that the SVI behaves just like a normal physical interface.

```
COM4 - PuTTY                                                    [_][□][X]
Switch#sh int vlan 501
Vlan501 is up, line protocol is up
  Hardware is EtherSVI, address is 6c41.6a24.20c2 (bia 6c41.6a24.20c2)
  Description: "User SVI"
  Internet address is 10.127.0.1/25
  MTU 1500 bytes, BW 1000000 Kbit/sec, DLY 10 usec,
     reliability 255/255, txload 1/255, rxload 1/255
  Encapsulation ARPA, loopback not set
  Keepalive not supported
  ARP type: ARPA, ARP Timeout 04:00:00
  Last input 00:00:01, output 00:00:37, output hang never
  Last clearing of "show interface" counters never
  Input queue: 0/75/0/0 (size/max/drops/flushes); Total output drops: 0
  Queueing strategy: fifo
  Output queue: 0/40 (size/max)
  5 minute input rate 0 bits/sec, 0 packets/sec
  5 minute output rate 0 bits/sec, 0 packets/sec
     7 packets input, 630 bytes, 0 no buffer
     Received 0 broadcasts (0 IP multicasts)
     0 runts, 0 giants, 0 throttles
     0 input errors, 0 CRC, 0 frame, 0 overrun, 0 ignored
     1 packets output, 64 bytes, 0 underruns
     0 output errors, 1 interface resets
--More--
```

Enabling IP Routing

To use SVIs or routed interfaces to perform routing functions on Layer 3 switches ip routing must be enabled using the following command:

```
(config)#ip routing
```

This allows a Layer 3 switch to forward traffic just like a router.

Configuring Trunk Ports

Trunk ports can transport data from multiple vlans through tagging packets with VLAN information. Some uses include connecting multiple switches together allowing the same vlans to be accessed across multiple switches, for wireless access points which need to broadcast SSIDs for multiple VLANs, or for virtual hosts whose VMs need access to multiple VLANs.

To create a trunk port the switch port must be configured in trunk mode and the encapsulation type must be specified. In this case we will be using IEEE 802.1Q, an open standard.

The native vlan is used for all untagged traffic, meaning if the switch receives a packet with no tagging it is assigned to the native vlan. The allowed vlan command allows only the specified VLANs to traverse the trunk. Industry wide practice is to explicitly specify the vlans which are allowed to prevent unauthorised traffic to travel across the trunk.

```
Switch(config)#int range gi 1/0/22-24
Switch(config-if-range)#description "Wireless AP Trunk"
Switch(config-if-range)#switchport trunk encapsulation dot1q
Switch(config-if-range)#switchport trunk native vlan 502
Switch(config-if-range)#switchport trunk allowed vlan 501,502,503,505
Switch(config-if-range)#switchport mode trunk
```

```
COM4 - PuTTY                                                          - □ X
Switch#
Switch#
Switch#
Switch#
Switch#
Switch#
Switch#
Switch#
Switch#
Switch#
Switch#
Switch#
Switch#
Switch#
Switch#config t
Enter configuration commands, one per line.  End with CNTL/Z.
Switch(config)#int range gi 1/0/22-24
Switch(config-if-range)#description "Wireless AP Trunk"
Switch(config-if-range)#switchport trunk encap dot1q
Switch(config-if-range)#switchport trunk native vlan 502
Switch(config-if-range)#switchport trunk allowed vlan 501,502,503,505
Switch(config-if-range)#switchport mode trunk
Switch(config-if-range)#exit
Switch(config)#
```

Voice Vlans

If you are using Cisco IP Phones, it is possible to create special trunk ports which allow a single ethernet cable to pass a data VLAN for clients and a Voice VLAN for phones. This is meant for access ports connected to Cisco phones.

To enable this feature, use the `(config-if)#switchport voice vlan` command on the interface. Notice in the configuration below one port is a member of two vlans without "being in trunk mode".

```
(config)# int gi 1/0/1
(config-if)# switchport access vlan 20
```

```
(config-if)# switchport mode access
(config-if)# switchport voice vlan 40
```

Power Over Ethernet (POE)

POE allows powering devices using ethernet cabling while still transmitting data. This technology is very useful for many applications, such as wireless access points (WAPs), security cameras, and VOIP phones. It can be very difficult and costly to run dedicated power to every device and POE allows a method to only run one cable instead of two.

There are two major POE standards, 802.3af and 802.3at sometimes known as POE+. The major difference between them is the maximum power delivered, at 15 Watts and 30 Watts, respectively.

To configure POE on switch ports, use the `(config-if)#power inline` command. By default, POE switch ports are set to autonegotiate power requirements with POE devices. If you would like to manually disable POE on a switch port, use the following command.

```
(config)# interface gi 0/1
(config-if)# power inline never
```

And to re enable it again:

```
(config)# interface gi 0/1
(config-if)# power inline auto
```

To view the status of POE on the switch, you can use the `#show power inline` command, which shows information such as the total and currently used power, as well as the POE devices connected to which port and their power draw. In the example below, you can see 3 generic POE devices using 4 Watts each, and a Cisco IP Phone 7961 using 6.3 Watts.

```
┌─────────────────────────────────────────────────────────────────────────────┐
│ ⟁                          10.124.0.1 - PuTTY                      –  □  ✕    │
├─────────────────────────────────────────────────────────────────────────────┤
│ Module   Available    Used      Remaining                                  ^ │
│          (Watts)      (Watts)   (Watts)                                       │
│ ------   ---------    --------  ---------                                     │
│ 1           525.0       55.4       469.6                                      │
│ 2           519.0       61.1       457.9                                      │
│ 3           500.0       57.9       442.1                                      │
│ Interface Admin  Oper      Power    Device               Class Max           │
│                            (Watts)                                            │
│ --------- ------ --------  -------  -------------------- ----- ----           │
│ Gi1/0/1   auto   off         0.0    n/a                   n/a   30.0          │
│ Gi1/0/2   auto   off         0.0    n/a                   n/a   30.0          │
│ Gi1/0/3   auto   off         0.0    n/a                   n/a   30.0          │
│ Gi1/0/4   auto   off         0.0    n/a                   n/a   30.0          │
│ Gi1/0/5   auto   off         0.0    n/a                   n/a   30.0          │
│ Gi1/0/6   auto   off         0.0    n/a                   n/a   30.0          │
│ Gi1/0/7   auto   off         0.0    n/a                   n/a   30.0          │
│ Gi1/0/8   auto   on          4.0    Ieee PD               1     30.0          │
│ Gi1/0/9   auto   on          4.0    Ieee PD               1     30.0          │
│ Gi1/0/10  auto   on          4.0    Ieee PD               1     30.0          │
│ Gi1/0/11  auto   off         0.0    n/a                   n/a   30.0          │
│ Gi1/0/12  auto   off         0.0    n/a                   n/a   30.0          │
│ Gi1/0/13  auto   on          6.3    IP Phone 7961         2     30.0          │
│ --More--  █                                                                 ∨ │
└─────────────────────────────────────────────────────────────────────────────┘
```

Spanning Tree Protocol (STP)

Spanning Tree Protocol is used to prevent layer 2 loops from forming between meshed switches. Loops are very dangerous as they are capable of bringing down an entire network by saturating links or overloading the CPU of switches. STP prevents loops by disabling redundant links, making sure there is only one path is active at any time. STP is enabled by default on Cisco switches, helping to protect against loops.

In the example below the redundant link to Switch 3 from Switch 2 is disabled via STP, preventing Layer 2 loops.

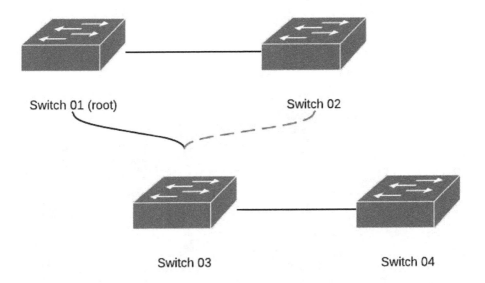

It is good practice to manually select which switch will be the root, as this switch will be doing the STP calculations for the entire network. The most powerful switch on the network, such as the core switches, would make prime candidates. If you do not select which switch will become root, the slowest, oldest switch on your network could be elected root!

The STP root is is elected by having the lowest bridge priority, and in the case of a tie, having the lowest mac address.To configure the spanning tree root primary and secondary, use the following commands:

```
(config)#spanning-tree vlan 1-4094 root primary
(config)#spanning-tree vlan 1-4094 root secondary
```

The above commands change the priority from default (32768) to 24576 (primary) and 28672 (secondary).

There are several STP protocols, with STP being the oldest. Other STP protocols include MST (Multiple Spanning Tree) and RPVST (Rapid Per-VLAN Spanning Tree). It is a good idea to enable RPVST on your switches, as it can greatly decrease convergence time from 30-60 seconds which are typical in STP.

```
(config)#spanning-tree mode rapid-pvst
```

Spanning tree functions by disabling a port while some time to test for loops when a device is first plugged in. This can be very annoying for your clients, as it may take 30-60 seconds to get a link after plugging into the network! A typical solution to this problem is by bypassing the STP check for access ports. This can be enabled with the portfast feature on the interface:

```
(config)#interface gi0/5
(config-if)#spanning-tree portfast
```

```
Switch(config)#
Switch(config)#
Switch(config)#
Switch(config)#
Switch(config)#
Switch(config)#
Switch(config)#
Switch(config)#
Switch(config)#
Switch(config)#
Switch(config)#
Switch(config)#
Switch(config)#
Switch(config)#
Switch(config)#int gi 0/5
Switch(config-if)#spanning-tree portfast
%Warning: portfast should only be enabled on ports connected to a single
 host. Connecting hubs, concentrators, switches, bridges, etc... to this
 interface  when portfast is enabled, can cause temporary bridging loops.
 Use with CAUTION

%Portfast has been configured on GigabitEthernet0/5 but will only
 have effect when the interface is in a non-trunking mode.
Switch(config-if)#
```

Cisco IOS warns you that using portfast can cause bridging loops. To help mitigate this issue, BPDU Guard can be used. BPDU guard checks a port for Bridge Protocol Data Units (BPDU), which are special packets used by spanning-tree. If one is detected, the port is disabled, and it will need to be manually re enabled later. This ensures no loops can be formed in the network.

To configure BPDU guard, use the command below:

```
(config-if)#spanning-tree bpduguard enable
```

Verifying Spanning Tree

The `#show spanning tree` command shows information about the STP root, the switch's STP configuration, and the STP status of the interfaces on the switch.

```
#show spanning-tree
```

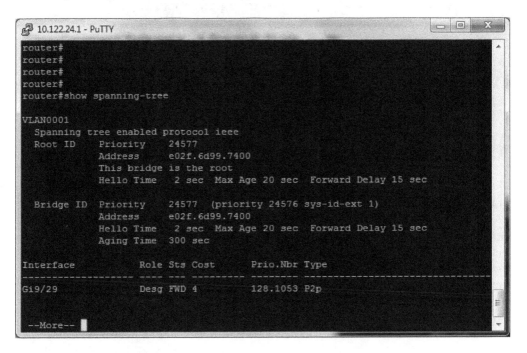

The #show spanning-tree summary command shows a brief overview of the STP status, such as the STP mode used, and the number of ports on each vlan in each STP state.

```
🖳 10.122.24.1 - PuTTY                                               _ ⊡ X
router#show spanning-tree summary
Switch is in pvst mode
Root bridge for: VLAN0001, VLAN0100, VLAN0110, VLAN0120, VLAN0124, VLAN0127
  VLAN0130, VLAN0140, VLAN0150, VLAN0160
Extended system ID          is enabled
Portfast Default            is disabled
PortFast BPDU Guard Default  is disabled
Portfast BPDU Filter Default is disabled
Loopguard Default           is disabled
EtherChannel misconfig guard is enabled
UplinkFast                  is disabled
BackboneFast                is disabled
Configured Pathcost method used is short

Name              Blocking Listening Learning Forwarding STP Active
---------------- -------- --------- -------- ---------- ----------
VLAN0001                0         0        0          1          1
VLAN0100                0         0        0          3          3
VLAN0110                0         0        0         16         16
VLAN0120                0         0        0         84         84
VLAN0124                0         0        0         44         44
VLAN0127                0         0        0          2          2
VLAN0130                0         0        0          5          5
 --More-- ▮
```

Vlan Trunking Protocol (VTP)

VLAN Trunking Protocol is a protocol developed to simplify the management of VLANs among multiple switches. A switch can be configured as a VTP server which allows all VTP clients to receive VLAN information automatically so it is not necessary to manually create VLANs on each switch.

All switches managed by VTP must be in the same VTP domain, they must be given a role (master, server, transparent, or off) and they can optionally be configured with a password.

```
S1(config)#vtp domain mydomain
S1(config)#vtp mode server
S1(config)#vtp password mypassword

S2(config)#vtp domain mydomain
S2(config)#vtp mode client
S2(config)#vtp password mypassword
```

TIP
Don't forget to configure trunk ports between the switches so they can pass vlan information via VTP.

```
S1(config)# interface gi 0/1
S1(config-if)#switchport trunk encapsulation dot1q
S1(config-if)#switchport mode trunk

S2(config)# interface gi 0/1
S2(config-if)#switchport trunk encapsulation dot1q
S2(config-if)#switchport mode trunk
```

Verifying VTP

The #show vtp status command gives an overview of the VTP process, including VTP version number, VTP mode, and VTP domain.

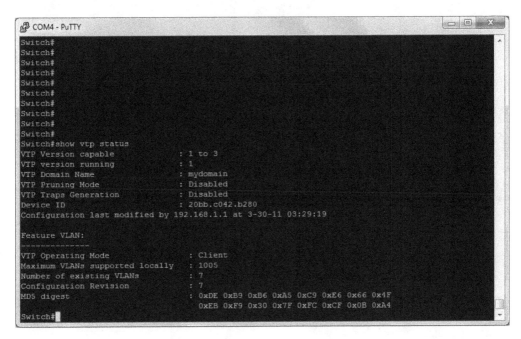

After creating vlan 66 and 77 on S1, the same VLANs show up automatically on S2! Check with the #show vlan command.

```
COM4 - PuTTY                                                             _ □ X
Switch#
Switch#
Switch#
Switch#sh vlan

VLAN Name                                Status    Ports
---- --------------------------------    --------- -------------------------------
1    default                             active    Gi0/1, Gi0/2, Gi0/4, Gi0/5
                                                   Gi0/6, Gi0/7, Gi0/8, Gi0/9
                                                   Gi0/10
66   vlans                               active
77   fun                                 active
1002 fddi-default                        act/unsup
1003 token-ring-default                  act/unsup
1004 fddinet-default                     act/unsup
1005 trnet-default                       act/unsup

VLAN Type  SAID      MTU   Parent RingNo BridgeNo Stp  BrdgMode Trans1 Trans2
---- ----- --------- ----- ------ ------ -------- ---- -------- ------ ------
1    enet  100001    1500  -      -      -        -    -        0      0
66   enet  100066    1500  -      -      -        -    -        0      0
77   enet  100077    1500  -      -      -        -    -        0      0
1002 fddi  101002    1500  -      -      -        -    -        0      0
1003 tr    101003    1500  -      -      -        -    srb      0      0
1004 fdnet 101004    1500  -      -      -        ieee -        0      0
1005 trnet 101005    1500  -      -      -        ibm  -        0      0

--More-- █
```

Link Aggregation (LAG)

Link Aggregation is used to combine multiple physical interfaces into one logical interface, increasing bandwidth and providing redundancy should one link fail. Because all ports are logically combined, redundant links within a LAG are not disabled via STP.

LAG is typically used to connect switches together on the backbone or for connecting high bandwidth servers such as virtual hosts or file servers to your network.

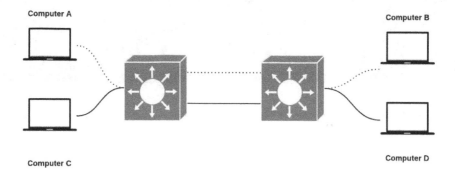

With LAG up to eight ports can be configured as one aggregated port. However, if we combine two 1gb ports we have an overall bandwidth of 2 gbps but the max throughput for any session is still just 1 gbps.

Why? Only one logical session can pass over a single link at any time. For example, Computer A can speak to Computer B using one of the aggregated links and at the same time Computer C can speak to Computer D on the other. One pair of computers can only use a single physical line in the port channel at any time but the overall bandwidth of the link is increased using LAG. If many sessions are passing along the LAG, they will be load balanced accordingly.

Configuring Link Aggregation and Control Protocol (LACP) requires two steps. First, a "port channel" must be configured. This is the new logical interface. Second, physical ports must be assigned to this logical interface.

Creating a port channel is very similar to configuring any other interface. Choose a number for your port channel between 1-64, in the example below I am using 11. In this example, the port channel is set up as a trunk port. It can also be set as a routed interface or even as an access port on a single VLAN.

```
(config)#interface port-channel 11
(config-if)#description "My Port Channel"
(config-if)#switchport
(config-if)#switchport trunk encap dot1q
(config-if)#switchport mode trunk
(config-if)#switchport trunk allowed vlan
100,110,120,124,130,140,150,160
(config-if)#switchport trunk native vlan 100
(config-if)#no shutdown
```

After the port channel has been configured, assign physical ports to it. In this case, I am adding two ten gigabit ethernet interfaces to the port channel.

```
(config)#int range te 1/1/3-4
(config-if)#description "Uplinks"
(config-if)#switchport
(config-if)#channel-group 11 mode on
(config-if)#no shutdown
```

Now we have two aggregated 10 gbps links for a total bandwidth of 20 gbps. This can help improve throughput and provides redundancy in case of a link failure on one of the lines.

Switch Stack Configuration (StackWise)

Several models of Cisco switches can be configured in "Switch Stacks". These stacks allow multiple physical switches to be combined into one logical unit for control and management.

On some systems proprietary "stackwise" cables like the ones shown below are used to connect multiple switches together. They are wired in typical daisy chain fashion, allowing up to nine members in a single stack. Check the cisco documentation for your model to see the cabling methodology. If any stackwise cable fails the switches can still communicate, but only at half bandwidth.

TIP
For best compatibility, stack members should be the same model and share the same IOS version.

In a switch stack, one unit is elected "master" and performs management tasks for the entire stack. By default, the switch with the lowest MAC address will be elected Master. To manually specify the master the priority value can be changed using the following command. Priority can be between 1 and 15, with 15 being the highest. The highest priority switch will be elected Master.

```
(config)#switch 1 priority 15
```

The #show switch command lists the switches currently in the stack, along with their priority value.

```
COM4 - PuTTY
Switch#
Switch#
Switch#config t
Enter configuration commands, one per line.  End with CNTL/Z.
Switch(config)#switch 1 priority 15
Changing the Switch Priority of Switch Number 1 to 15
Do you want to continue?[confirm]
New Priority has been set successfully

Switch(config)#exit
Switch#
Mar 30 01:31:20.230: %SYS-5-CONFIG_I: Configured from console by console
Switch#show sw
Switch#show switch
Switch/Stack Mac Address : acf2.c51f.f700
                                    H/W   Current
Switch#  Role   Mac Address     Priority Version State
-----------------------------------------------------------
*1       Master acf2.c51f.f700     15      3       Ready
 2       Member bc16.65e0.0500     1       3       Ready

Switch#
```

Sometimes switches in a stack need to be renumbered. By default, the switches are numbered from lowest to highest MAC address. Because of this, you could end up with switch 3 at the top, switch 1 in the middle, and switch 2 on the bottom of the physical stack! For your own sanity, its probably easier to have them logically configured the same way they are physically set up.

To renumber a switch, simply execute the following command. In this example, we are changing switch number 1 to switch number 3.

```
(config)# switch 1 renumber 3
```

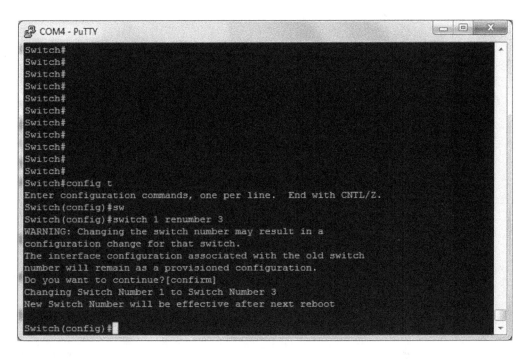

```
COM4 - PuTTY                                                    — ▢ ✕

Switch#
Switch#
Switch#
Switch#
Switch#
Switch#
Switch#
Switch#
Switch#
Switch#
Switch#
Switch#config t
Enter configuration commands, one per line.  End with CNTL/Z.
Switch(config)#sw
Switch(config)#switch 1 renumber 3
WARNING: Changing the switch number may result in a
configuration change for that switch.
The interface configuration associated with the old switch
number will remain as a provisioned configuration.
Do you want to continue?[confirm]
Changing Switch Number 1 to Switch Number 3
New Switch Number will be effective after next reboot

Switch(config)#
```

The switch number reassignment takes place after the next reboot.

Virtual Switching System (VSS)

VSS is another system of combining two physical switches into one logical unit. It is available on higher end cisco switches and only supports two switches. Unlike Stackwise both switches must be configured to support it, not just the master. Instead of using Stackwise cables typical copper or fiber ethernet connections are used to make the connection between the units.

Like with Stackwise, when using VSS you can create LAGs (port channel's) across two switches. This allows you to have redundancy that would otherwise not be possible. Without VSS, links to one switch would be put into blocking mode by STP. In this scenario links to both switches can pass traffic at the same time, and if a physical switch fails you can ensure you still have connectivity as long as your downstream equipment is physically cabled to both VSS switches.

To configure VSS, you must first assign both units to the same Virtual Domain. In the virtual domain section, you must also assign a number to the switch, such as Switch 1 for the first and Switch 2 for the second. On the interface that will be connecting the units together (A port-channel, in the example below) you must enter the (config-if)#switch virtual link 1 command. Lastly, the stitches must be converted to VSS mode using the (config)#switch `convert mode virtual` command. After the command has been executed, the switches will reboot and they will act as one logical unit!

To return the switches to stand alone units, use the `(config)#switch convert mode stand-alone` command.

TIP
Configuration can only be done from the primary switch, so make sure you are consoling into the primary when making configuration changes. The standby console will prevented from making any configuration changes.

VSS Lab

Switch 1 Configuration

```
S1(config)#switch virtual domain 100
S1(config-vs-domain)#switch 1
!
S1(config)#interface port-channel 1
S1(config-if)#switchport
S1(config-if)#switch virtual link 1
S1(config-if)#no shutdown
S1(config-if)#exit
!
S1(config)#int range te 1/13-16
S1(config-if-range)#description "VSS Link"
S1(config-if-range)#channel-group 1 mode on
S1(config-if-range)#no shutdown
!
S1(config)#switch convert mode virtual
```

Switch 2 Configuration

```
S2(config)#switch virtual domain 100
S2(config-vs-domain)#switch 2
!
S2(config)#interface port-channel 2
S2(config-if)#switchport
S2(config-if)#switch virtual link 2
S2(config-if)#no shutdown
S2(config-if)#exit
!
S2(config)#int range te 1/13-16
S2(config-if-range)#description "VSS Link"
```

```
S2(config-if-range)#channel-group 2 mode on
S2(config-if-range)#no shutdown
!
S2(config)#switch convert mode virtual
```

To view the status of the VSS, you can use the `#show switch virtual` command which shows you information about the active and standby switches.

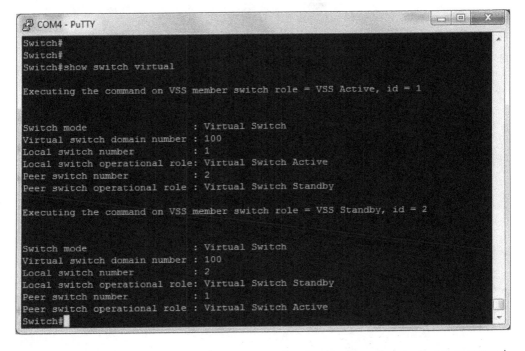

To reload both switches at once use the `(config)#redundancy reload shelf` command. You can also choose to reload only the peer, if required. The normal reload command will only reload the primary unit, causing the second switch to be promoted to active.

Chapter 5 - Routing

Routing Basics

It is always necessary for traffic to know the correct path to traverse while travelling to its destination. Choosing this path through a network is known as *routing*. There are two main methods for a Network Administrator to set up these paths.

Static vs Dynamic Routing

Static Routing, which is set manually by the administrator, and *Dynamic Routing*, which uses routing protocols to automatically create optimal routes and modify them when there is a change in the network layout.

Static routing is the simplest method and is an great introduction to the topic. Dynamic Routing will be covered in this section by protocol - namely RIP, EIGRP, OSPF, and BGP.

Interior vs Exterior Gateway Protocols

RIP, EIGRP, and OSPF are internal gateway protocols, meaning they are used inside an Autonomous System (AS), such as a collection of corporate LANs.

RIP is an older protocol and is not typically used in production unless absolutely necessary due to its many limitations, but it is a great precursor to understanding the more complex protocols. EIGRP is a Cisco Proprietary routing protocol which is scalable and easy to use. OSPF is an open protocol which is supported by nearly all vendors, is equally scalable, but can be more complex to configure and understand.

BGP by contrast is an exterior gateway protocol, which is extremely scalable and is used as the routing protocol of the public internet. Exterior gateway protocols are used to share routing information between Autonomous Systems, or isolated routing domains. BGP scales very well (for example, to the size of the public internet) and has powerful metrics, but is very slow to converge and is lacking common features of IGPs such as automatic peer detection.

Distance Vector vs Link State

Distance vector protocols such as RIP are sometimes known as "routing by rumor" because each router learns routing information from their neighbors only. Each router shares their full routing table with their neighbors. Because they cannot see more than one hop away, a router does not know where its neighbor learned its route. In essence, they have limited knowledge about the topology of the network..

R1	R2	R3

192.168.50.0/24   10.100.0.0/24   172.20.0.0/24   192.168.200.0/24

In the example above, if R1-R3 are using a distance vector routing protocol, R1 would learn 172.20.0.0/24 and 192.160.200.0/24 from R2. If something were to happen to R3, R1 would still try to pass information there via R2 until R2 lets R1 know that there is an issue!

Link state protocols such as OSPF function instead by having each router calculate the best paths independently, in contrast with distance vector routing protocol such as RIP and EIGRP which function through sharing full routing routing tables with their neighbors. With link state protocols all routers in a routing domain share their directly connected network information with all others. Because each router has a full view of the network, each router can *independently* calculate the the best routes!

Administrative Distance

To help prevent confusion on routers running multiple protocols, Cisco uses a value called administrative distance. If multiple routes to the same location are present from multiple routing protocols, AD is used to determine which route will be installed in the routing table.

Below are the default administrative distances for major routing protocols. For example, a route learned by EIGRP will be prefered over the same route learned by OSPF.

TIP
It is important to note that administrative distance is only considered for identical routes from two or more routing protocols. Otherwise the normal rule is followed, the most specific route is chosen. For example, if a route learned by OSPF is more specific than a route learned by EIGRP, it will be preferred to that destination even though it has a higher AD.

Routing Protocol	AD
Directly connected interface	0

Static route out an interface	1
Static route to next-hop address	1
EIGRP summary route	5
External BGP	20
Internal EIGRP	90
OSPF	110
IS-IS	115
Routing Information Protocol (RIP)	120
External EIGRP	170
Internal BGP	200

Static Routing

Creating a static route is a snap using the `(config)#ip route` command. Static routes can be configured using either the next hop ip address for the traffic, or the interface of the router the traffic should traverse to get to its destination.

The basic syntax of the command is `(config)#ip route` *destination network subnet mask next-hop address*

For example:

```
(config)#ip route 192.168.1.0 255.255.255.0 192.168.0.1
```

The above command adds a static route to the routing table. It instructs the router to send data destined to 192.168.1.0/24 via 192.168.0.1.

You can also specify a next hop interface instead of an IP address. For example, you can send all traffic destined for 192.168.1.0/24 out interface FastEthernet0/1.

```
(config)#ip route 192.168.1.0 255.255.255.0 FastEthernet0/1
```

Default Routes

A default route is used as a last resort when no other route exists in the routing table. Default routes are usually used at the edge of your network to reach the public internet, or on stub routers - routers which only have one connection into and out of your network.

Configuring a defualt route is very similar to configuring other static routes, only the destination address is configured as 0.0.0.0 with subnet mask 0.0.0.0 - this is known as the default route, indicating all possible locations.

The basic syntax is:

```
(config)#ip route 0.0.0.0 0.0.0.0 192.168.0.1
```

or

```
(config)#ip route 0.0.0.0 0.0.0.0 GigabitEthernet0/1
```

Verifying Routes

To check the routes currently in the routing table, you can use the `#show ip route` command. The routing table is the current set of rules that determine the destination of traffic.

How to read the route table

The `#show ip route` command can list routes installed from many sources, like static routes, RIP routes, or BGP routes. There are codes used to help you understand where the routes are coming from. For example, C denotes directly connected networks, R denotes RIP routes, and

B denotes BGP routes. In addition, there are many other types of routes which we will go over in this section.

```
Router#
Router#
Router#
Router#
Router#
Router#
Router#
Router#
Router#
Router#
Router#
Router#sh ip route
Codes: L - local, C - connected, S - static, R - RIP, M - mobile, B - BGP
       D - EIGRP, EX - EIGRP external, O - OSPF, IA - OSPF inter area
       N1 - OSPF NSSA external type 1, N2 - OSPF NSSA external type 2
       E1 - OSPF external type 1, E2 - OSPF external type 2
       i - IS-IS, su - IS-IS summary, L1 - IS-IS level-1, L2 - IS-IS level-2
       ia - IS-IS inter area, * - candidate default, U - per-user static route
       o - ODR, P - periodic downloaded static route, H - NHRP, l - LISP
       + - replicated route, % - next hop override

Gateway of last resort is not set

Router#
```

Routing Information Protocol (RIP)

Routing Information Protocol (RIP), is a distance vector routing protocol. It uses hop count to determine the best route to a destination. Given two paths to a destination RIP will choose the shortest, regardless of other concerns such as bandwidth or delay. RIP would choose to take a shorter path over a T1 circuit, rather than a longer path using Ten Gigabit fiber!

One of the major limitations of RIP is that the maximum number of hops supported is 15. The farthest a packet can travel is through 15 routers. This may have been acceptable when networks were small, but it is very limiting in modern environments.

RIP also sends full route table updates to its peers every 30 seconds. This creates overhead on the network - imagine the inefficiency of sharing a routing table with 100,000 routes every 30 seconds, regardless of any changes!

RIP Configuration

To configure RIP on your network, use the `(config)# router rip` command. This puts you into RIP configuration mode. After entering this mode, specify the networks you would like to advertise via RIP using the `(config-router)# network x.x.x.x` command.

You can also specify the version of RIP to run, v1 or v2 by using the `(config-router)# version 2` command. RIPv1 does not support classless routing and Version 1 is enabled by default. Because most modern networks are classless, it is best to enable RIP v2.

```
(config)# router rip
(config-router)# network 192.168.1.0
(config-router)# version 2
```

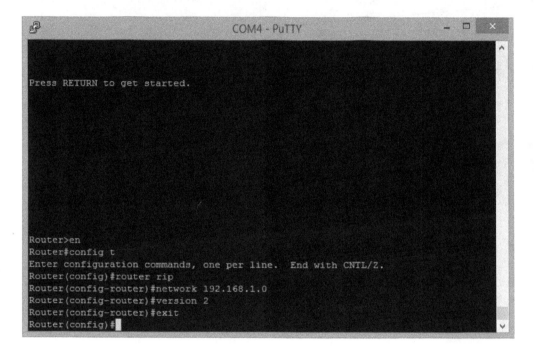

RIP is enabled all interfaces by default. To manually prevent routing updates to be sent out an interface, use the passive interface command:

```
(config-router)# passive interface gi 0/0
```

You can also choose to make all interfaces passive by default and manually enable the interfaces which you would like to send routing updates. You can do this with the following commands:

```
(config-router)# passive interface default
```

```
(config-router)# no passive interface gi 0/1
```

RIP usually sends routing updates via broadcasts. If RIP needs to be configured on nonbroadcast networks, you can send unicast packets to a neighbor by specifying it with the neighbor command.

```
(config-router)# neighbor x.x.x.x
```

To prevent RIP from auto summarizing routes into classful boundaries, use the no auto summary command. This prevents a router connected to 172.16.1.0/24 and 172.16.130.0/24 to advertise a connection to the class B network 172.16.0.0/16 to its neighbors - instead advertising the seperate /24 networks. Auto summarization creates many issues and it best to disable it in most situations, unless the network has been designed specifically for its use.

```
(config-router)# no auto-summary
```

If you would like to advertise the default route (0.0.0.0/0) via RIP, use the default information originate command.

```
(config-router)# default information originate
```

RIP Lab

The image below shows a simple network which we will configure with RIP in the quick example below. We must enable RIP, add the network statements, enable version 2, and verify our results.

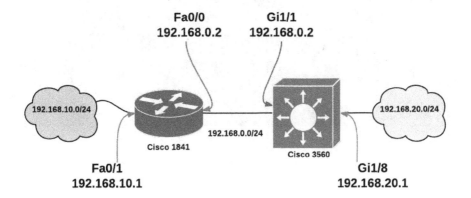

1841 RIP Configuration

```
R1(config)# router rip
R1(config-router)# network 192.168.0.0
R1(config-router)# network 192.168.10.0
R1(config-router)# version 2
```

3560 RIP Configuration

```
S1(config)# ip routing
S1(config)# router rip
S1(config-router)# network 192.168.0.0
S1(config-router)# network 192.168.20.0
S1(config-router)# version 2
```

The output of the show ip route command on 1841 shows the route 192.168.20.0 was learned from 3560 via RIP (R)!

```
┌─────────────────────── COM4 - PuTTY ───────────── - □ ✕ ┐
Router#
Router#
Router#sh ip route
Codes: L - local, C - connected, S - static, R - RIP, M - mobile, B - BGP
       D - EIGRP, EX - EIGRP external, O - OSPF, IA - OSPF inter area
       N1 - OSPF NSSA external type 1, N2 - OSPF NSSA external type 2
       E1 - OSPF external type 1, E2 - OSPF external type 2
       i - IS-IS, su - IS-IS summary, L1 - IS-IS level-1, L2 - IS-IS level-2
       ia - IS-IS inter area, * - candidate default, U - per-user static route
       o - ODR, P - periodic downloaded static route, H - NHRP, l - LISP
       + - replicated route, % - next hop override

Gateway of last resort is not set

      192.168.0.0/24 is variably subnetted, 2 subnets, 2 masks
C        192.168.0.0/24 is directly connected, FastEthernet0/0
L        192.168.0.2/32 is directly connected, FastEthernet0/0
S     192.168.1.0/24 [1/0] via 192.168.0.1
                     is directly connected, FastEthernet0/1
      192.168.10.0/24 is variably subnetted, 2 subnets, 2 masks
C        192.168.10.0/24 is directly connected, FastEthernet0/1
L        192.168.10.1/32 is directly connected, FastEthernet0/1
R     192.168.20.0/24 [120/1] via 192.168.0.1, 00:00:24, FastEthernet0/0
Router#
```

EIGRP

EIGRP (Enhanced Interior Gateway Routing Protocol) is a proprietary routing protocol developed by Cisco Systems. Technically, Cisco has opened EIGRP as an open standard in 2013, but it has not yet see widespread support outside of Cisco equipment. It is an advanced distance-vector routing protocol which has proven to be very scalable and relatively simple to configure.

Metrics

EIGRP has multiple metrics in addition to hop count to make routing decisions, unlike RIP which only uses hop count. The metrics are configured via "k values" listed below:

1. Bandwidth
2. Load
3. Delay
4. Reliability

By default, the EIGRP best path calculation only includes bandwidth and delay, but the others can be enabled by modifying the k values.

Successors

EIGRP uses the concept of successors (the most direct route) and feasible successors (suitable routes to a destination that are guaranteed to not cause routing loops but are not the most direct). Successors are installed in the routing table, and feasible successors are ready to be injected into the routing table if the successor becomes unavailable.

EIGRP Configuration

Like with RIP, you must enable the EIGRP process using the `(config)# router` command. Unlike RIP, you must also specify an autonomous system number - all routers exchanging EIGRP routing information must share this same number AS number. This example shows configuring EIGRP with AS number 10.

```
(config)# router EIGRP 10
```

Networks to be advertised are added using the `(config-router)#network` command, just like RIP.

```
(config-router)# network 192.168.10.0 255.255.255.0
```

TIP
It a good idea to enable logging of neighbor changes - this can be very helpful when troubleshoot EIGRP issues.

```
(config-router)#eigrp log-neighbor-changes
```

Modifying metrics (k values) allows tweaking the operation of EIGRP to your needs. It is important to note that EIGRP neighbors need to share the same metrics to become neighbors.

Below is the formula EIGRP uses to determine its metric, the k values can be modified using the metric weights command also shown below.

```
metric = [K1*bandwidth + (K2*bandwidth)/(256 - load) + K3*delay] *
[K5/(reliability + K4)]

(config-router)#metric weights tos k1 k2 k3 k4 k5
```

Note: Cisco documentation states that TOS (type of service) must always be zero.

Default routes need to be statically redistributed into EIGRP, there is no analog to the default-information originate command. To advertise the static route, first create the route and then use the redistribute static command. Note this will add *all the static routes* on the router to be advertised via EIGRP!

```
(config)#ip route 0.0.0.0 0.0.0.0 1.2.3.4
(config)#router eigrp 10
(config-router)#redistribute static
```

Like RIP, EIGRP auto summarises to classful boundaries by default. In most situations this is undesirable, you can disable it using the following command:

```
(config-router)# no auto-summary
```

The passive interface and neighbor commands function similar to RIP. Check out that section for details.

EIGRP Lab

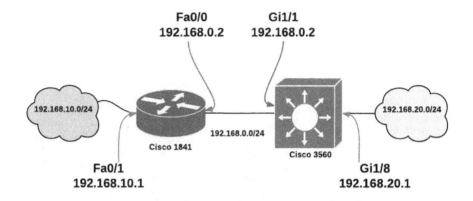

Fa0/0
192.168.0.2

Gi1/1
192.168.0.2

192.168.10.0/24

192.168.0.0/24

192.168.20.0/24

Cisco 1841

Cisco 3560

Fa0/1
192.168.10.1

Gi1/8
192.168.20.1

Using the same network as the RIP exercise, lets configure EIGRP.

1841 Configuration

```
R1(config)# router eigrp 10
R1(config-router)# network 192.168.0.0 255.255.255.0
R1(config-router)# network 192.168.10.0 255.255.255.0
R1(config-router)# eigrp log-neighbor-changes
R1(config-router)# no auto-summary
```

3560 Configuration

```
S1(config)# router eigrp 10
S1(config-router)# network 192.168.0.0 255.255.255.0
S1(config-router)# network 192.168.20.0 255.255.255.0
S1(config-router)# eigrp log-neighbor-changes
S1(config-router)# no auto-summary
```

The commands were very similar to RIP, weren't they? Let's verify our results with the show ip route command. On 1841 we can see the 192.168.20.0/24 route advertised via 3560 using EIGRP (D)!

```
COM4 - PuTTY                                                    _  □  ✕

Router#
Router#
Router#sh ip route
Codes: L - local, C - connected, S - static, R - RIP, M - mobile, B - BGP
       D - EIGRP, EX - EIGRP external, O - OSPF, IA - OSPF inter area
       N1 - OSPF NSSA external type 1, N2 - OSPF NSSA external type 2
       E1 - OSPF external type 1, E2 - OSPF external type 2
       i - IS-IS, su - IS-IS summary, L1 - IS-IS level-1, L2 - IS-IS level-2
       ia - IS-IS inter area, * - candidate default, U - per-user static route
       o - ODR, P - periodic downloaded static route, H - NHRP, l - LISP
       + - replicated route, % - next hop override

Gateway of last resort is not set

      192.168.0.0/24 is variably subnetted, 2 subnets, 2 masks
C        192.168.0.0/24 is directly connected, FastEthernet0/0
L        192.168.0.2/32 is directly connected, FastEthernet0/0
S     192.168.1.0/24 [1/0] via 192.168.0.1
                     is directly connected, FastEthernet0/1
      192.168.10.0/24 is variably subnetted, 2 subnets, 2 masks
C        192.168.10.0/24 is directly connected, FastEthernet0/1
L        192.168.10.1/32 is directly connected, FastEthernet0/1
D     192.168.20.0/24 [90/28416] via 192.168.0.1, 00:00:51, FastEthernet0/0
Router#
```

To verify our EIGRP neighbors, we can use the following command:

```
#show ip eigrp neighbors
```

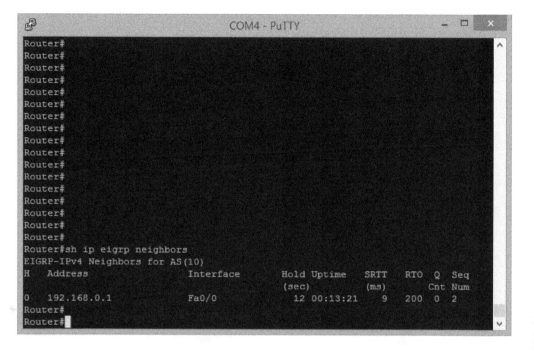

OSPF

Unlike EIGRP, OSPF (Open Shortest Path First) is a link state routing protocol. By using Link State Advertisements (LSAs), each router on the network independently calculates the best route to each destination.

OSPF is an open standard meaning it can be used on equipment from nearly all vendors.

It uses the concept of Areas, or localised routing domains. This allows summarization at area boundaries, effectively forcing network architects into good network design practices. By creating localised routing domains, summarization can be performed at the boundaries helping to prevent routing tables from growing too large.

All areas must connect to the backbone area, Area 0. However, if an area cannot directly connect to Area 0 it is possible to create a "virtual link" through an intermediate area back to area 0.

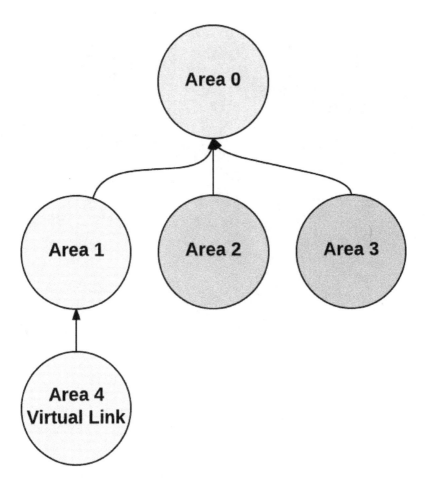

Routers which have all their interfaces in a single area are are called Internal Routers (**IRs**). A router that connect an area to the backbone is called an Area Border Router (**ABR**). A router that is running multiple routing protocols and is redistributing external routes into OSPF are called Autonomous system boundary routers (**ASBRs**).

Based on network type, a router may be elected Designated Router (**DR**) or Backup Designated Router (**BDR**) - these routers form neighbor relationships with all other routers on the network. All other routers, which are not DRs or BDRs are known as **DROTHERs**. Some networks, like point to point links, do not elect DRs and BDRs because there are only two routers participating.

In networks with DRs and BDRs, the BDR is a hot standby in case of a failure of the DR. The DR alleviates the need for all routers to form neighbor relationships with each other - as long as a router can talk to the DR it will learn all the routes from its peers.

By default, the router with the highest router ID is elected DR. You can also increase the priority from the default 1 to a maximum of 255 on the router's interface to ensure it is elected DR on that segment, using the following command:

```
(config-if)#ip ospf priority 10
```

OSPF cost is calculated using a reference bandwidth of 100 Mbps. For example, in the case of Ethernet, the cost is 100 Mbps / 10 Mbps = 10. That means that Fast Ethernet, Gigabit Ethernet, and Ten Gigabit Ethernet all have the same cost of 1! That means OSPF treats all these links as the same. To solve this issue, you can change the reference bandwidth, or the bandwidth setting of the interface.

OSPF Neighbor States

OSPF exchanges information using OSPF packets. These packets allow OSPF neighbors to share their Link State databases, request link state updates, and ensure all OSPF neighbors have the same LSA information.

- Hello
- Database Description (DBD)
- Link State Request (LSR)
- Link State Update (LSU)
- Link State Acknowledgement (LSAck)

While forming neighbors, OSPF routers go through many states. Only routers in the Full state have established adjacencies. If a neighbor is stuck in any other state, the adjacency has not formed, most likely due to incorrect configuration. These OSPF states are walked through sequentially as a new router establishes communication with its DR, exchanges databases, and finally has the same database as all it's peers.

- Down
- Attempt
- INIT
- Two Way
- Exstart
- Exchange
- Loading
- Full

OSPF routers go through these states while forming neighborship status. To become neighbors, their configurations must match. Some of the attributes which must be the same between neighbors are:

- Routers must be in the same area
- They must use the same hello and dead timers (10 and 40 seconds, by default)
- They must have the same interface MTU
- They must be the same network type (Broadcast, Point to Point, NBMA, etc)

Link State Advertisements (LSAs) and Area Types

As noted above, OSPF is a Link state protocol. It functions through sharing routing information with all other routers in the same OSPF area. There are several types of OSPF Areas, the most typical of which are shown below:

Backbone - The center of the OSPF network, Area 0
Standard - Normal Areas which do not fall in any other category
Stub - Routing from within the area is based on a default route, there is only one path out
Not So Stubby Area (NSSA) - Like a stub but allows importing and exporting of routes external to the AS

Different types of LSAs are used for sharing different types of information. Below are the common LSA types.

Type 1 - A list of directly attached links (comes from each router)
Type 2 - A list of all routers on the network (comes from the DR)
Type 3 - A list of all routes in an area (used by ABRs to share routes between areas)
Type 4 - Routes to ASBRs
Type 5 - A list of all routes in another AS (used by ASBRs to share routes between ASs)
Type 7 - Used in stub areas instead of type 5 LSAs for external routes

To see the OSPF Database which contains LSA information, use the #show ip ospf database command.

In the first example below, we see a few different LSAs. We recieved two type 1 LSAs from 10.123.16.100 and 10.127.250.3, our peers in this area. The Type 2 LSA comes from the ID of the DR, 10.123.16.100. The Type 3 LSA for this area is is 0.0.0.0, the default route, because this is a stub area.

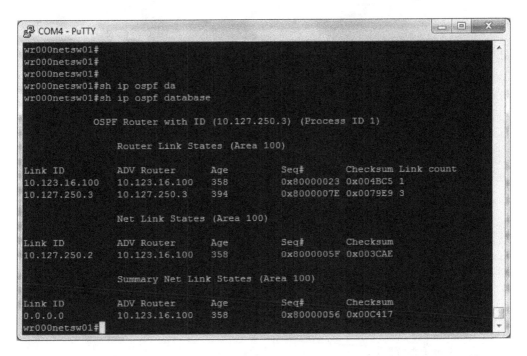

```
COM4 - PuTTY                                                              ─ □ X

wr000netsw01#
wr000netsw01#
wr000netsw01#
wr000netsw01#sh ip ospf da
wr000netsw01#sh ip ospf database

            OSPF Router with ID (10.127.250.3) (Process ID 1)

            Router Link States (Area 100)

Link ID           ADV Router        Age       Seq#         Checksum Link count
10.123.16.100     10.123.16.100     358       0x80000023 0x004BC5 1
10.127.250.3      10.127.250.3      394       0x8000007E 0x0079E9 3

            Net Link States (Area 100)

Link ID           ADV Router        Age       Seq#         Checksum
10.127.250.2      10.123.16.100     358       0x8000005F 0x003CAE

            Summary Net Link States (Area 100)

Link ID           ADV Router        Age       Seq#         Checksum
0.0.0.0           10.123.16.100     358       0x80000056 0x00C417
wr000netsw01#
```

In the second example below we see a standard area. We see Type 1 LSAs from three routers in the area, 10.127.224.17, 10.127.224.18, and 10.127.224.18. The Type 2 LSA comes from the DR, 10.127.224.17. Next we see several Type 5 external LSAs, which are external routes injected into OSPF from ASBRs.

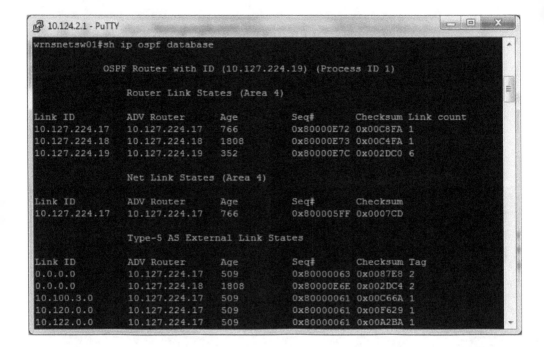

```
10.124.2.1 - PuTTY                                                  □  x
wrnsnetsw01#sh ip ospf database

           OSPF Router with ID (10.127.224.19) (Process ID 1)

              Router Link States (Area 4)

Link ID          ADV Router       Age       Seq#        Checksum Link count
10.127.224.17    10.127.224.17    766       0x80000E72 0x00C8FA 1
10.127.224.18    10.127.224.18    1808      0x80000E73 0x00C4FA 1
10.127.224.19    10.127.224.19    352       0x80000E7C 0x002DC0 6

              Net Link States (Area 4)

Link ID          ADV Router       Age       Seq#        Checksum
10.127.224.17    10.127.224.17    766       0x800005FF 0x0007CD

              Type-5 AS External Link States

Link ID          ADV Router       Age       Seq#        Checksum Tag
0.0.0.0          10.127.224.17    509       0x80000063 0x0087E8 2
0.0.0.0          10.127.224.18    1808      0x80000E6E 0x002DC4 2
10.100.3.0       10.127.224.17    509       0x80000061 0x00C66A 1
10.120.0.0       10.127.224.17    509       0x80000061 0x00F629 1
10.122.0.0       10.127.224.17    509       0x80000061 0x00A2BA 1
```

OSPF Configuration

Just like RIP and EIGRP, OSPF must be configured using the `(config)#router` command. Unlike RIP or EIGRP, you must also specify a process ID. This has local significance only and each number represents a separate OSPF process.

Like other dynamic routing protocols, you must add the network statement to specify which networks are added to the OSPF process. Unlike the other protocols, you must also specify the area number for the route.

TIP
Its is very important to remember area information is defined per interface, not per router. A router with three interfaces could be in three different areas!

The syntax of the OSPF network command is: `(config)#network x.x.x.x y.y.y.y area z`, where X is the subnet address, Y is the wildcard mask, and Z the the area number, between 0 and 4294967295.

TIP
Note that OSPF uses wildcard masks and not subnet masks in its network statement.

This example shows configuring OSPF process 1 with a network in area 0.

```
(config)# router OSPF 1
(config-router)# network 192.168.1.0 0.0.0.255 area 0
```

By default the router ID used by the OSPF process is the highest IP address configured on the system, with a preference for loopback addresses. Thus, if a loopback address is configured on the system, the highest loopback IP address will be selected. The router ID is shown in the neighbor table and OSPF database, and is used for DR election. To make troubleshooting easier, you may wish to manually specify the router id with the following command:

```
(config-router)# router-id 192.168.1.1
```

Like RIP, the OSPF routing process can also advertise default routes. To do so use the following command:

```
(config-router)# default-information originate
```

To specify which router will be elected DR, it is possible to change the priority value. By default, the router with the highest ID will become DR. A priority of 255 is the most likely to become DR, and a priority of 0 means that the router will never become DR.

```
(config-router)# priority 1
```

You may wish to change the hello and dead timers, which determine the amount of time that can pass without communication to determine if a neighbor is down. Lowering these values can decrease convergence time.

The hello timer is how often the router checks to see if its neighbor is still responding. The dead timer is how much time must pass before a neighbor is considered down. By default on broadcast multiaccess networks (such as ethernet), the dead timer is 4 times the hello timer, which are 40 and 10 seconds respectively.

To change these attributes, use the following commands on the interfaces running OSPF. Remember, all neighbors must share the same hello and dead timers.

```
(config-if)#ip ospf hello-interval 5
(config-if)#ip ospf dead-interval 20
```

To log neighbor adjacency changes, you can use the `(config-router)# log-adjacency-changes` command. This can be very helpful when troubleshooting.

The passive interface and neighbor commands function similar to RIP. Check out that section for details.

OSPF Lab

We will configure our test network again, this time using multi area OSPF. The two routers will connect over the backbone area 0, and advertise their respective networks which are in area 10 and 20, respectively. In this design the routers will be acting as ABRs, and 1841 will be the DR.

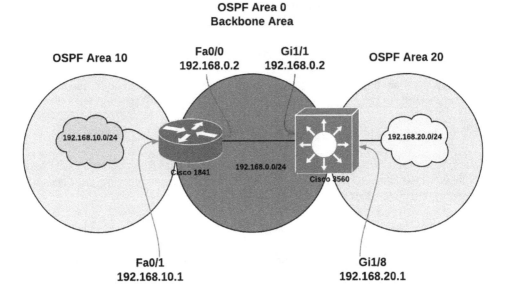

1841 Configuration

```
R1(config)# router ospf 1
R1(config-router)# network 192.168.0.0 0.0.0.255 area 0
R1(config-router)# network 192.168.10.0 0.0.0.255 area 10
R1(config-router)# router-id 192.168.0.2
R1(config-router)# priority 1
R1(config-router)# log-adjacency-changes
```

3560 Configuration

```
S1(config)# router ospf 1
S1(config-router)# network 192.168.0.0 0.0.0.255 area 0
S1(config-router)# network 192.168.20.0 0.0.0.255 area 20
S1(config-router)# router-id 192.168.0.1
S1(config-router)# log-adjacency-changes
```

On 1841 we can see the 192.168.20.0/24 route advertised via 3560 using OSPF Inter Area (IA)! If we had just used area 0 everywhere we would have seen this route advertised as a normal OSPF route (O) instead.

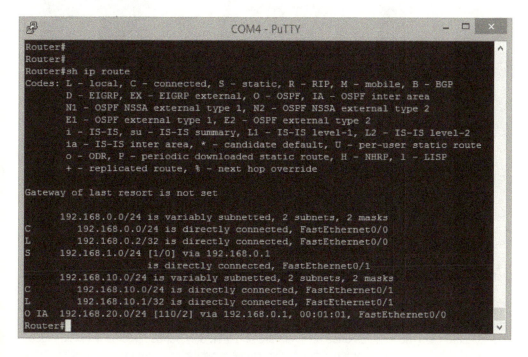

```
Router#
Router#
Router#sh ip route
Codes: L - local, C - connected, S - static, R - RIP, M - mobile, B - BGP
       D - EIGRP, EX - EIGRP external, O - OSPF, IA - OSPF inter area
       N1 - OSPF NSSA external type 1, N2 - OSPF NSSA external type 2
       E1 - OSPF external type 1, E2 - OSPF external type 2
       i - IS-IS, su - IS-IS summary, L1 - IS-IS level-1, L2 - IS-IS level-2
       ia - IS-IS inter area, * - candidate default, U - per-user static route
       o - ODR, P - periodic downloaded static route, H - NHRP, l - LISP
       + - replicated route, % - next hop override

Gateway of last resort is not set

      192.168.0.0/24 is variably subnetted, 2 subnets, 2 masks
C        192.168.0.0/24 is directly connected, FastEthernet0/0
L        192.168.0.2/32 is directly connected, FastEthernet0/0
S     192.168.1.0/24 [1/0] via 192.168.0.1
                     is directly connected, FastEthernet0/1
      192.168.10.0/24 is variably subnetted, 2 subnets, 2 masks
C        192.168.10.0/24 is directly connected, FastEthernet0/1
L        192.168.10.1/32 is directly connected, FastEthernet0/1
O IA  192.168.20.0/24 [110/2] via 192.168.0.1, 00:01:01, FastEthernet0/0
Router#
```

We can verify our neighbor information using the #show ip ospf neighbor command. This command is very useful when troubleshooting OSPF neighborship issues.

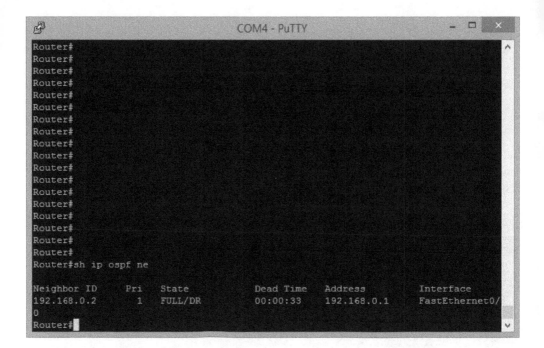

```
Router#
Router#
Router#
Router#
Router#
Router#
Router#
Router#
Router#
Router#
Router#
Router#
Router#
Router#
Router#
Router#
Router#
Router#sh ip ospf ne

Neighbor ID     Pri   State          Dead Time   Address        Interface
192.168.0.2      1    FULL/DR        00:00:33    192.168.0.1    FastEthernet0/
0
Router#
```

BGP

BGP is an exterior gateway routing protocol which is used to exchange routing information between Autonomous Systems (ASs). Typically IGPs such as OSPF or EIGRP are used within ASs and BGP is used to connect these ASs together.

BGP is designed to scale to extremely large networks, such as the public internet. It is known as as "path vector" protocol, determining best path based on the fewest ASs crossed.

Unlike EIGRP or OSPF which use their own Layer 4 protocols, BGP runs over TCP on port 179. BGP synchronises route tables once upon startup and then only sends updates when changes are made. This helps limit communication between peers, which helps improve scalability. To verify neighbors are still up keepalives are periodically sent.

BGP is very powerful due to making routing decisions based on many configurable metrics. Some of these metrics are shown below:

1. Weight
2. Local Preference
3. Multi Exit Discriminator
4. Origin
5. AS Path

6. Next Hop
7. Community

At its simplest, the shortest AS path is preferred, assuming other metrics are the same.

Like other routing protocols, there are multiple states in which BGP peers go through on the way to to forming full neighbor status. Once the neighbor is configured, it is entered into the idle state. It sends packets to its neighbor and enters the Open Sent state. If no reply is received within 5 seconds, the router enters the Active state, which is an error state. If a response is received, the two peers become Established and can begin to share routing information.

BGP states
- Idle
- Connect
- Open Sent
- Active - Error State
- Open Confirm
- Established

There are two types of BPG - external BGP (eBGP) and internal BGP (iBGP). External BGP is used between different ASs. Internal BGP is used inside a single AS.

eBGP is typically used to connect your organization to two or more ISPs or for ISPs or large organizations to peer together. Using BGP with two ISPs allows advertising a single network block across multiple ISPs. This way an IP address range can be reachable from multiple ISPs - so in the case of a failure of one ISP link the IP address will still be reachable to the world through the other.

This also allows traffic entering or exiting your network to intelligently choose the best path between your two ISPs, for example it may be less hops to reach a client from your network over ISP 1 rather than ISP 2! As you can imagine, this can really improve performance through intelligent load sharing.

BGP ISP Connection Types

When connecting to multiple ISPs, there are many methods to choose from to determine how you wish to learn BGP routes.

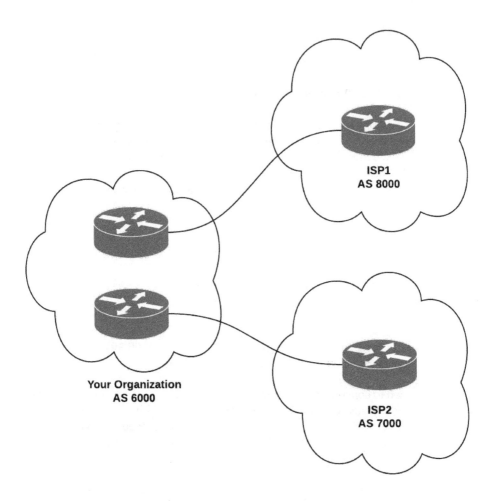

ISP1
AS 8000

Your Organization
AS 6000

ISP2
AS 7000

The simplest method is to have your ISPs send you a static default route - 0.0.0.0/0. This mitigates most advantages gained from using BGP, as you cannot intelligently select the best path. However, because you are advertising your networks to your ISPs, this method allows for your network IPs to be reached from multiple ISPs.

Second, you can receive partial BGP table updates as well as a default route. For example, an ISP can share all of the routes on that ISPs network only in addition to a default route. Using this method you can choose the best path for networks directly attached to one of your ISPs. This allows you to have many of the benefits of BGP without having to have very expensive equipment capable of running full BGP tables.

The last option is to have ISPs send the entire BGP routing table, around 540k routes at the time of writing, to be shared with you. This allows you to choose the best route to all locations on the internet, but it requires powerful and expensive routers to handle the workload.

TIP
You can check out tons of information about the global status of BGP, including total number of routes, the owner of AS numbers, and more from http://www.cidr-report.org/

BGP Configuration

eBGP and iBGP are configured in the same manner. The main difference is that in iBGP the AS number of the local router and remote router are the same.

TIP
Unlike the internal gateway protocols, there is no method for automatic neighbor detection. Neighbors must be manually configured.

In the configuration below our router in AS 100 is running eBGP with 5.5.5.5 in AS 101.

```
(config)#router bgp 100
(config-router)#network 1.0.0.0
(config-router)#network 2.0.0.0
(config-router)#neighbor 5.5.5.5 remote-as 101
```

A simple loop detection mechanism exists in eBGP. To prevent loops from forming in eBGP, a router will not accept any updates including their own Autonomous System number. Meaning it will not accept a route that it itself sourced.

There are a few extra things to keep in mind when using iBGP.

iBGP peers must be fully meshed. This can cause serious scaling problems as the number of links required for a fully meshed network increases rapidly at n(n-1)/2. Luckily, this issue can be resolved with two methods - through using a route reflector or using BGP Confederations.

Confederations allows you to break your iBGP AS into multiple sub ASs, which communicate via eBGP. This helps ease the full mesh requirement.

Route Reflectors allow iBGP peers to communicate to one central location which reflects the routes to all other iBGP routers.

The configuration of iBGP with route reflectors is very simple. Each of the "spokes" needs only to have a neighbor statement pointing to the reflector. The only difference on the reflector side is using the `(config-router)# neighbor x.x.x.x route-reflector-client` command.

An example BGP route reflector configuration would look like this:

```
(config)#router bgp 65000
(config-router)#network 1.0.0.0
(config-router)#network 2.0.0.0
(config-router)#neighbor 7.7.7.7 remote-as 65000
(config-router)# neighbor 7.7.7.7 route-reflector-client
(config-router)#neighbor 9.9.9.9 remote-as 65000
(config-router)# neighbor 9.9.9.9 route-reflector-client
```

Thats it!

TIP
Remember, you can configure multiple route reflectors for redundancy. Simply have the "spoke" routers be neighbors with all route reflectors.

eBGP Lab

Basic configuration of eBGP is fairly straight forward. BGP is configured using the
`(config)#router bgp` command. You must also specify the local AS number in the router statement.

In the example below we specify two routers in AS 65000 and 65001, respectively. Notice we must specify the neighbor manually, this is because BGP has no neighbor discovery mechanism unlike EIGRP or OSPF. We can tell this is an eBGP configuration because the local AS and remote AS are different. The network statement should now look familiar from the other routing protocols we've studied.

```
R1(config)#router bgp 65000
R1(config-router)#neighbor 10.0.0.2 remote-as 65001
R1(config-router)#network 192.168.10.0 mask 255.255.255.0

R2(config)#router bgp 65001
R2(config-router)#neighbor 10.0.0.1 remote-as 65000
R2(config-router)#network 192.168.20.0 mask 255.255.255.0
```

To check the status of the BGP route table, use the `#show ip bgp` command. The ">" character in the table shows the best route to the destination, if many are available.

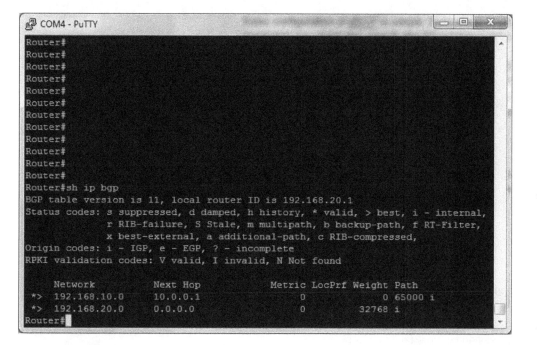

Only the best routes are installed in the route table. Below, we see the 192.168.10.0/24 network sared via BGP (B)!

```
COM4 - PuTTY

Router#
Router#
Router#
Router#
Router#sh ip route
Codes: L - local, C - connected, S - static, R - RIP, M - mobile, B - BGP
       D - EIGRP, EX - EIGRP external, O - OSPF, IA - OSPF inter area
       N1 - OSPF NSSA external type 1, N2 - OSPF NSSA external type 2
       E1 - OSPF external type 1, E2 - OSPF external type 2
       i - IS-IS, su - IS-IS summary, L1 - IS-IS level-1, L2 - IS-IS level-2
       ia - IS-IS inter area, * - candidate default, U - per-user static route
       o - ODR, P - periodic downloaded static route, H - NHRP, l - LISP
       + - replicated route, % - next hop override

Gateway of last resort is not set

      10.0.0.0/8 is variably subnetted, 2 subnets, 2 masks
C        10.0.0.0/24 is directly connected, GigabitEthernet0/0
L        10.0.0.2/32 is directly connected, GigabitEthernet0/0
B     192.168.10.0/24 [20/0] via 10.0.0.1, 00:13:05
      192.168.20.0/24 is variably subnetted, 2 subnets, 2 masks
C        192.168.20.0/24 is directly connected, GigabitEthernet0/1
L        192.168.20.1/32 is directly connected, GigabitEthernet0/1
Router#
```

iBGP Lab with Loopbacks

Now we will look at configuring iBGP. At its simplest, the process is the same as eBGP but the local and remote AS numbers are the same.

In this configuration we will be using loopback addresses for creating BGP neighbors. Why? If a physical interface on a router goes down, BGP will not be able to communicate. However, as long as one path exists the loopback interface will remain available. This allows the BGP session to be more fault tolerant.

To use a loopback interface for BGP, we must first create the interface. A loopback interface is configured in the same way as a physical interface. To specify this interface is to be used for bgp, you must use the `update-source` keyword under the neighbor statement in the configuration.

```
(config-router)#neighbor 172.16.0.2 update-source loopback 0
```

When using iBGP, routers will advertise the IP address of the eBGP peer they learned a route from. Meaning, an iBGP router will always use this address, even if the next iBGP peer cannot reach it! Imagine 3 routers in a line R1 > R2 > R3. By default, R2 will advertise eBGP routes learned by R1 using R1s address, but R3 cannot reach R1 directly!

To resolve this issue, R2 can be set to advertise its own IP address as the next hop by using the `next-hop-self` command.

We'll illustrate both of these concepts in the lab below.

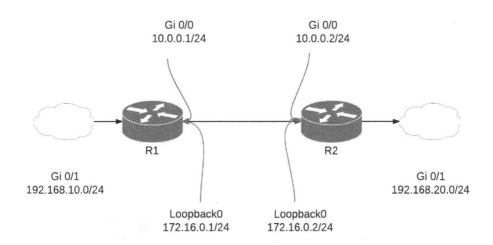

Router 1 Configuration

```
R1(config)#int loopback 0
R1(config-if)#ip address 172.16.0.1 255.255.255.0
R1(config-if)#no shutdown
!
R1(config)#router bgp 65000
R1(config-router)#neighbor 172.16.0.2 remote-as 65000
R1(config-router)#neighbor 172.16.0.2 update-source loopback 0
R1(config-router)#neighbor 172.16.0.2 next-hop-self
R1(config-router)#network 192.168.10.0 mask 255.255.255.0
!
R1(config)#ip route 172.16.0.2 255.255.255.255 10.0.0.2
```

Router 2 Configuration

```
R2(config)#int loopback 0
R2(config-if)#ip address 172.16.0.2 255.255.255.0
R2(config-if)#no shutdown
!
R2(config)#router bgp 65000
```

```
R2(config-router)#neighbor 172.16.0.1 remote-as 65000
R2(config-router)#neighbor 172.16.0.1 update-source loopback 0
R2(config-router)#neighbor 172.16.0.1 next-hop-self
R2(config-router)#network 192.168.20.0 mask 255.255.255.0
!
R2(config)#ip route 172.16.0.1 255.255.255.255 10.0.0.1
```

After creating the loopback and changing the update source, we have successfully created a bgp neighborship!

Lets verify that the routes are learned correctly.

```
#show ip route
```

We see the correct route installed via the loopback address of our peer!

Chapter 6 - Wide Area Networks (WANs)

It is often necessary to connect several physically separate locations together allowing private traffic to travel between them. There are many technologies capable of achieving this ranging from direct connections via dark fiber, to managed solutions through an ISP such as MPLS, or creating tunnels over the public internet.

In this section we will explore several configurations of the last type. Namely, GRE, IPsec, and a combination of the two.

Introduction to VPN Tunneling

VPN (virtual Private Network) Tunnels allow private networks to communicate over the public internet. Users will be able to access private resources at remote sites the same way they access local resources - and the process is completely transparent to them.

This is achieved using VPN protocols such as those mentioned above. VPN protocols function by encapsulating data inside a new packet, modifying the packet headers to allow the packet to traverse the public internet.

A private IP address such as those in the 10.0.0.0/24 CIDR block cannot be routed over the internet. To send it over the internet the original packet is placed inside a new packet, this new packet using the public IP address of the local gateway as its source and the public IP address of the remote gateway as its destination. This new packet can be sent over the internet just like any other. When the remote gateway receives this packet, it strips off the public IP address headers and reveals the original packet, passing it on to another private address.

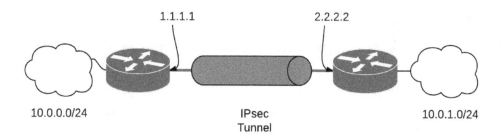

1.1.1.1   2.2.2.2

10.0.0.0/24   IPsec Tunnel   10.0.1.0/24

In the image above, a packet traveling from the private IP address 10.0.0.0/24 going to 10.0.1.0/24 will be encapsulated inside a packet with the public IP source address 1.1.1.1 and destination address 2.2.2.2. Once 2.2.2.2 receieves the packet, it will strip the public IP information and pass the packet on to the private 10.0.1.0/24 network.

Generic Routing Encapsulation (GRE)

GRE or Generic Routing Encapsulation is a tunneling protocol originally developed by Cisco to encapsulate traffic over the internet. Since it has become an open standard and sees widespread support from nearly all vendors.

It is a very simple protocol, offering bare bones tunneling and little else. It is capable of encapsulating many network layer protocols, although it is typically used to encapsulate IP packets.

GRE does not encryption - anyone can read the content of the packets. For that reason it is typically inadvisable to use over the public internet on its own. For use on the internet, it is often combined with IPsec to offer high levels of security and flexibility, which will be covered later in this section.

GRE Tunnel Configuration

Configuring GRE on Cisco IOS is simple, which makes it a great place to start when studying encapsulation.

To establish a GRE tunnel between two Cisco routers it is necessary to create a Tunnel Interface. This is a virtual interface which serves as the endpoint for the VPN tunnel. It is configured and behaves in the same manner as physical interfaces.

The tunnel interface in our example is using private address space. These addresses are the tunnel endpoints, which are logically linked to the public IP addresses of the gateways. You can just think of them as hops along the private network.

Under the Tunnel1 interface, you must specify the tunnel source and destination, using the `(config-if)#tunnel source` and `(config-if)#tunnel destination` commands respectively.

The tunnel source is on the public side of the router. It can be either an IP address or a physical interface. For R1 below, I specified the interface gi0/0, but it is equally valid to specify the interface's public ip address of 206.111.121.170. The tunnel destination is the public IP address of the peer gateway, 69.163.56.156.

TIP

The `(config-if)#ip mtu 1400` command is extremely important. This command alters the MTU or Maximum Transferable Unit, which is the maximum Layer 2 packet size that can be transferred over this link. This is so important because now that we are encapsulating traffic we are introducing new packet headers, which in turn increase overall packet size.

If we do not decrease this value from its default of 1500 bits, packet fragmentation may take place due to this new overhead. When a packet is fragmented it is broken into two or more packets.

Packet fragmentation can cause terrible performance due to the overhead of breaking up and recombining packets. It may even prevent the link from functioning at all, as many routers on the internet are programmed to discard fragmented packets as a security measure. This is because many Denial of Service (DoS) attacks use large numbers of tiny fragmented packets to overload a system, so many network administrators program their devices to discard them.

It may be necessary to decrease this number to even less than 1400 depending on the minimum MTU configured on the path between the two endpoints. This minimum MTU along the path can be found using Path MTU Discovery (PMTUD).

GRE Lab

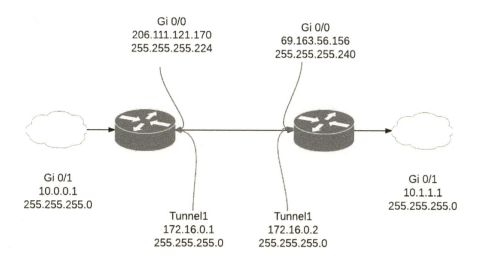

In our example network above, Gi 0/0 is the public facing interface, Gi 0/1 is the private facing interface and Tunnel1 is the Virtual Tunnel Interface which terminates the GRE tunnel.

In the lab below we are going to create a GRE tunnel between these two hosts. We will be using static routing as our routing mechanism for this example, but you could use a dynamic routing protocol instead.

R1 Configuration

```
R1(config)#interface GigabitEthernet0/0
R1(config-if)#no shutdown
R1(config-if)#ip address 206.111.121.170 255.255.255.224
!
R1(config)#interface GigabitEthernet0/1
R1(config-if)#no shutdown
R1(config-if)#ip address 10.0.0.1 255.255.255.0
!
R1(config)#ip route 0.0.0.0 0.0.0.0 206.111.121.161
R1(config)#ip route 10.1.1.0 255.255.255.0 172.16.0.2
!
R1(config)#interface Tunnel1
R1(config-if)#ip address 172.16.0.1 255.255.255.0
R1(config-if)#ip mtu 1400
R1(config-if)#tunnel source gi0/0
R1(config-if)#tunnel destination 69.163.56.156
```

R2 Configuration

```
R2(config)#interface GigabitEthernet0/0
R2(config-if)#no shutdown
R2(config-if)#ip address 69.163.56.156 255.255.255.240
!
R2(config)#interface GigabitEthernet0/1
R2(config-if)#no shutdown
R2(config-if)#ip address 10.1.1.1 255.255.255.0
!
R2(config)#ip route 0.0.0.0 0.0.0.0 69.163.56.145
R1(config)#ip route 10.0.0.0 255.255.255.0 172.16.0.1
!
R2(config)#interface Tunnel1
R2(config-if)#ip address 172.16.0.2 255.255.255.0
R2(config-if)#ip mtu 1400
R2(config-if)#tunnel source gi0/0
R2(config-if)#tunnel destination 206.111.121.170
```

Test this configuration by pinging a remote private IP address from a local private IP address. For example, from 10.0.0.2 to 10.1.1.2. If the traffic can pass, you have successfully configured the tunnel!

Internet Protocol Security (IPsec)

IPsec or Internet Protocol Security is a group of protocols for securing IP communications via encryption, authentication, and integrity checks.

IPsec can encrypt data making it unreadable by anyone but the intended recipient. It also provides authentication, cryptographically proving the identity of the sender and receiver. And lastly it provides data integrity, verifying data has not been altered in transit.

IPsec has two main protocols, Authentication Header (AH) and Encapsulating Security Payload (ESP).

AH provides authentication and integrity checks only, it does not encrypt traffic.

ESP provides encryption, authentication, and integrity checks and is typically used for site to site tunnels due to the addition of cryptographic security.

IPsec can operate in two main modes - Transport mode and Tunnel mode.

Transport Mode encrypts only the payload of the IP packet, leaving the IP header untouched.

Tunnel Mode encrypts the entirety of the packet, including the IP header. This mode can be used to create IPsec tunnels, allowing private networks to communicate over the public internet.

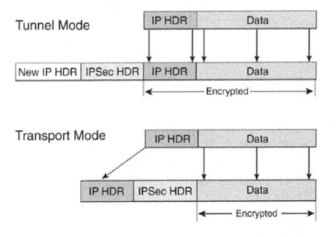

IPsec is established in two phases using ISAKMP (Internet Security Association and Key Management Protocol). ISAKMP establishes "Security Associations" (SAs) between peers. SAs are shared security attributes agreed upon between two peers.

In phase 1 ISAKMP uses asymmetric cryptography to create a secure channel. This channel is used in phase 2 to negotiate the symmetric encryption keys which will be used for bulk file transfer.

Both ends of the IPsec connection must agree upon these phase 1 and phase 2 parameters to successfully communicate.

Asymmetric cryptography uses unique encryption keys on both both ends of the connection, meaning the key used to encrypt data is different than the key used to decrypt it. This allows verifying the authenticity of both sides of the connection, as only they know their encryption key. Assuming secrecy of the private keys is maintained, asymmetric cryptography is extremely secure.

But asymmetric cryptography is also very computationally intensive. Because of this, most encryption schemes (such as IPsec and SSL) use a hybrid model. Asymmetric cryptography is used to agree upon a symmetric key. This symmetric key is used for bulk file transfer, as it is much less resource intensive and symmetric cryptography is also very secure as long as the symmetric key remains secret.

Cryptography is a very broad topic and could fill a book by itself. I suggest further reading to study the specifics of encryption algorithms, hashing algorithms, and other related topics.

IPsec Tunnel Configuration

First we will explore configuring IPsec in Tunnel mode, creating an encrypted site to site tunnel. To create an IPsec tunnel, we must define the phase 1 and phase 2 ISAKMP attributes.

Phase 1 Attributes:

Below is an example of configuring phase 1 ISAKMP attributes. These are the encryption attributes used when initially establishing the tunnel using asymmetric cryptography.

First we create a numbered isakmp policy, in this case we arbitrarily choose the number 10. This number is only locally significant. This is followed by the cipher used (AES 256), the hashing algorithm used (SHA 256), the authentication type (pre shared key), and the diffie hellman (group14). The diffie hellman group determines the strength of the key used during the key exchange process. Common DH groups are shown below.

DH Group 1: 768-bit group
DH Group 2: 1024-bit group

DH Group 5: 1536-bit group
DH Group 14: 2048-bit group
DH Group 15: 3072-bit group
DH Group 19: 256-bit elliptic curve group
DH Group 20: 384-bit elliptic curve group

To specify the pre shared key, use the `(config)#crypto isakmp key xxx network wildcard_mask` command. In this example the key is "testkey" and we are allowing connections from all IP addresses (0.0.0.0/0).

TIP
Although we will not be covering it in this book, it is also possible to use RSA keys instead of PSKs for phase 1 negotiation.

```
crypto isakmp policy 10
encryption aes 256
hash sha256
auth pre-share
group 14
!
crypto isakmp key testkey address 0.0.0.0 0.0.0.0
```

Phase 2 Attributes:

Next we must configure the phase 2 parameters. These are the encryption attributes for the bulk data transfer phase.

To define the phase 2 attributes, which are a combination of security protocols and algorithms, use the `(config)#crypto ipsec transform-set` command.

In this case, we named the transform set "myset" and defined the cypher and mode used (esp-aes 256), meaning ESP mode using the AES 256 cipher. Lastly, we define the hashing algorithm used (esp-sha-hmac).

```
(config)#crypto ipsec transform-set myset esp-aes 256 esp-sha-hmac
```

TIP
You can use the "?" operator with the `(config)#crypto ipsec transform-set` command to see many other cypher and hashing options. At the time of writing, AES 256 and SHA are considered good options for strong security.

We can also use an ACL to limit what traffic will be encrypted via IPsec. A simple example is shown below, which permits the 192.168.0.0/16 private address space to be encrypted via IPsec when traversing to any other private network.

```
(config)#access-list 101 permit ip 192.168.0.0 0.0.255.255 10.0.0.0
0.255.255.255
(config)#access-list 101 permit ip 192.168.0.0 0.0.255.255 192.168.0.0
0.0.255.255
(config)#access-list 101 permit ip 192.168.0.0 0.0.255.255 172.16.0.0
0.15.255.255
```

Lastly, we create a "crypto map" to combine all these attributes together. In the example below, the crypto map is named "mymap" and numbered 10. It is also defined as an IPsec-ISAKMP type crypto map.

Here we set our IPsec peer (50.74.110.93), define our phase 2 attributes by referencing our transform set (myset), and specify which traffic this crypto map applies to (ACL 101).

```
crypto map mymap 10 ipsec-isakmp
set peer 50.74.110.93
set transform-set myset
match address 101
```

Once we have created our phase 1 configuration, phase 2 configuration, access control list, and crypto map we can apply this crypto map to an interface to activate it.

```
(config)#interface GigabitEthernet0/0
(config-if)#crypto map mymap
```

IPsec Tunnel Lab

IPsec is a complex protocol. Look over the notes above and build out the lab below to test these concepts out for yourself. It may take a little bit to grasp all the concepts! In this lab be will be using the network diagram below.

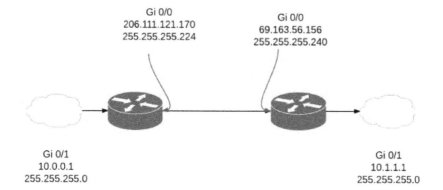

Gi 0/0
206.111.121.170
255.255.255.224

Gi 0/0
69.163.56.156
255.255.255.240

Gi 0/1
10.0.0.1
255.255.255.0

Gi 0/1
10.1.1.1
255.255.255.0

Router 1 Configuration

```
R1(config)#interface GigabitEthernet0/0
R1(config-if)#no shutdown
R1(config-if)#ip address 206.111.121.166 255.255.255.224
R1(config-if)#crypto map mymap
!
R1(config)#interface GigabitEthernet0/1
R1(config-if)#no shutdown
R1(config-if)#ip address 192.168.10.1 255.255.255.0
!
R1(config)#ip route 0.0.0.0 0.0.0.0 206.111.121.161
!
R1(config)#crypto isakmp policy 10
R1(config-isakmp)#encryption aes 256
R1(config-isakmp)#hash sha256
R1(config-isakmp)#auth pre-share
R1(config-isakmp)#group 14
R1(config)#exit
R1(config)#crypto isakmp key testkey address 0.0.0.0 0.0.0.0
!
R1(config)#crypto ipsec transform-set myset esp-aes 256 esp-sha-hmac
R1(config)#exit
!
R1(config)#access-list 101 permit ip 192.168.0.0 0.0.255.255 10.0.0.0
0.255.255.255
R1(config)#access-list 101 permit ip 192.168.0.0 0.0.255.255
192.168.0.0 0.0.255.255
```

```
R1(config)#access-list 101 permit ip 192.168.0.0 0.0.255.255
172.16.0.0 0.15.255.255
!
R1(config)#crypto map mymap 10 ipsec-isakmp
R1(config-crypto-map)#set peer 50.74.110.93
R1(config-crypto-map)#set transform-set myset
R1(config-crypto-map)#match address 101
R1(config)#exit
!
```

Router 2 Configuration

```
R2(config)#interface GigabitEthernet0/0
R2(config-if)#no shutdown
R2(config-if)#ip address 50.74.110.93 255.255.255.248
R2(config-if)#crypto map mymap
!
R2(config)#interface GigabitEthernet0/1
R2(config-if)#no shutdown
R2(config-if)#ip address 192.168.20.1 255.255.255.0
!
R2(config)#ip route 0.0.0.0 0.0.0.0 50.74.110.89
!
R2(config)#crypto isakmp policy 10
R2(config-isakmp)#encryption aes 256
R2(config-isakmp)#hash sha256
R2(config-isakmp)#auth pre-share
R2(config-isakmp)#group 14
R2(config)#exit
R2(config)#crypto isakmp key testkey address 0.0.0.0 0.0.0.0
!
R2(config)#crypto ipsec transform-set myset esp-aes 256 esp-sha-hmac
R2(config)#exit
!
R2(config)#access-list 101 permit ip 192.168.0.0 0.0.255.255 10.0.0.0
0.255.255.255
R2(config)#access-list 101 permit ip 192.168.0.0 0.0.255.255
192.168.0.0 0.0.255.255
R2(config)#access-list 101 permit ip 192.168.0.0 0.0.255.255
172.16.0.0 0.15.255.255
!
R2(config)#crypto map mymap 10 ipsec-isakmp
R2(config-crypto-map)#set peer 206.111.121.166
R2(config-crypto-map)#set transform-set myset
R2(config-crypto-map)#match address 101
```

```
R2(config)#exit
```

GRE over IPsec

IPsec in Tunnel mode is very powerful - it allows two sites to communicate over the public internet privately. However, it has a major limitation; multicast traffic cannot traverse IPsec tunnels. Because of this limitation, traffic that depends on multicast, such as most dynamic routing protocols, cannot work over IPsec Tunnels.

This is a serious limitation, as dynamic routing protocols are very powerful tools in a Network Engineer's repertoire. One solution to this problem is combining GRE and IPsec, leveraging the power of each.

TIP
GRE has no limitations concerning multicast traffic, but it does not support encryption. IPsec transport mode offers terrific encryption, but does not support tunneling. One solution to this problem is using GRE for tunneling and leveraging IPsec transport mode for encryption.

Remember that IPsec transport mode does not modify the IP headers, leaving routing information intact, but it does allow for complete end to end encryption. With this method it is possible to have your cake and eat it too, end to end encryption and multicast traffic enabled at the same time!

The configuration for GRE over IPSEC uses many of the same concepts from above. We create a tunnel interface just like in our GRE lab, and we create ISAKMP phase 1 and phase 2 attributes just like in our IPsec Tunnel lab. The major difference lies in the IPsec mode used - note that we are using Transport Mode in this example instead of Tunnel Mode (the default).

The example below uses static routing for simplicity, but a dynamic routing protocol could be used to share the 192.168.X.X routes instead.

GRE over IPsec Lab

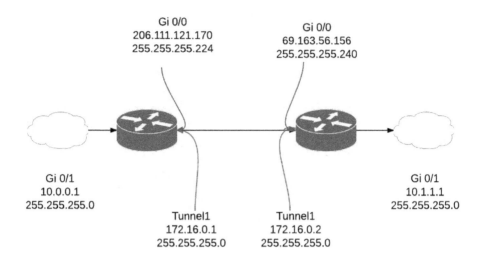

Router 1

```
R1(config)#interface GigabitEthernet0/0
R1(config-if)#no shutdown
R1(config-if)#ip address 50.74.110.93 255.255.255.248
R1(config-if)#crypto map mymap
!
R1(config)#interface GigabitEthernet0/1
R1(config-if)#no shutdown
R1(config-if)#ip address 192.168.20.1 255.255.255.0
!
R1(config)#interface Tunnel1
R1(config-if)#ip address 172.16.0.2 255.255.255.0
R1(config-if)#tunnel source gi0/0
R1(config-if)#tunnel destination 206.111.121.166
!
R1(config)#crypto isakmp policy 10
R1(config-isakmp)#encryption aes 256
R1(config-isakmp)#hash sha256
R1(config-isakmp)#auth pre-share
R1(config-isakmp)#group 14
!
R1(config)#crypto isakmp key testkey address 206.111.121.166
!
R1(config)#crypto ipsec transform-set myset esp-aes 256 esp-sha-hmac
R1(config)#mode transport
!
```

```
R1(config)#crypto map mymap 10 ipsec-isakmp
R1(config-crypto-map)#set peer 206.111.121.166
R1(config-crypto-map)#set transform-set myset
R1(config-crypto-map)#match address vpnendpoints
!
R1(config)#ip route 0.0.0.0 0.0.0.0 50.74.110.89
R1(config)#ip route 192.168.10.0 255.255.255.0 172.16.0.1
!
R1(config)#ip access-list extended vpnendpoints
R1(config)#permit gre any any
```

Router 2

```
R2(config)#interface GigabitEthernet0/0
R2(config-if)#no shutdown
R2(config-if)#ip address 206.111.121.166 255.255.255.248
R2(config-if)#crypto map mymap
!
R2(config)#interface GigabitEthernet0/1
R2(config-if)#no shutdown
R2(config-if)#ip address 192.168.10.1 255.255.255.0
!
R2(config)#interface Tunnel1
R2(config-if)#ip address 172.16.0.1 255.255.255.0
R2(config-if)#tunnel source gi0/0
R2(config-if)#tunnel destination 50.74.110.93
!
R2(config)#crypto isakmp policy 10
R2(config-isakmp)#encryption aes 256
R2(config-isakmp)#hash sha256
R2(config-isakmp)#auth pre-share
R2(config-isakmp)#group 14
!
R2(config)#crypto isakmp key testkey address 50.74.110.93
!
R2(config)#crypto ipsec transform-set myset esp-aes 256 esp-sha-hmac
R2(config)#mode transport
!
R2(config)#crypto map mymap 10 ipsec-isakmp
R2(config-crypto-map)#set peer 50.74.110.93
R2(config-crypto-map)#set transform-set myset
R2(config-crypto-map)#match address vpnendpoints
!
R2(config)#ip route 0.0.0.0 0.0.0.0 50.74.110.89
```

```
R2(config)#ip route 192.168.20.0 255.255.255.0 172.16.0.2
!
R2(config)#ip access-list extended vpnendpoints
R2(config)#permit gre any any
```

Troubleshooting IPsec

To verify that IPsec is functioning correctly, you can check the ISAKMP and IPSEC Security Associations (SA). The following commands will tell you the status of your phase 1 or phase 2 negotiations.

To see the status of the phase 1 negotiation, use the following command:

```
#show crypto isakmp sa
```

In the example below, Router Test2 has an ISAKMP SA with another router in the QM_IDLE state, meaning the SA is correctly established.

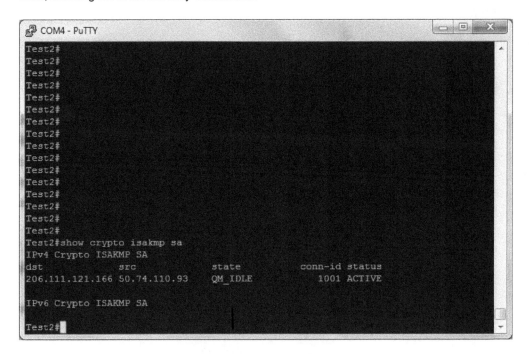

To view the phase 2 status, use the following command:

```
#show crypto ipsec sa
```

In the example below we see an SA between the 192.168.0.0/16 and the 192.168.0.0/16 networks. Notice that we see 489 encapsulated packets and 488 de-encapsulated packets. This illustrates that packets are being successfully encrypted and unencrypted across the connection!

```
COM4 - PuTTY                                              [ - ] [ □ ] [ X ]
Test2#show crypto ipsec sa

interface: GigabitEthernet0/0
    Crypto map tag: mymap, local addr 50.74.110.93

  protected vrf: (none)
  local  ident (addr/mask/prot/port): (192.168.0.0/255.255.0.0/0/0)
  remote ident (addr/mask/prot/port): (192.168.0.0/255.255.0.0/0/0)
  current_peer 206.111.121.166 port 500
    PERMIT, flags={origin_is_acl,}
   #pkts encaps: 489, #pkts encrypt: 489, #pkts digest: 489
   #pkts decaps: 488, #pkts decrypt: 488, #pkts verify: 488
   #pkts compressed: 0, #pkts decompressed: 0
   #pkts not compressed: 0, #pkts compr. failed: 0
   #pkts not decompressed: 0, #pkts decompress failed: 0
   #send errors 0, #recv errors 0

    local crypto endpt.: 50.74.110.93, remote crypto endpt.: 206.111.121.166
    path mtu 1500, ip mtu 1500, ip mtu idb GigabitEthernet0/0
    current outbound spi: 0xF0410F54(4030795604)
    PFS (Y/N): N, DH group: none

    inbound esp sas:
     spi: 0xBEE2296E(3202492782)
```

If the above commands are showing that there are problems, it may be time to use debugging features of cisco IOS. These commands will output a large amount of detailed data about the ISAKMP phase 1 and phase 2 negotiations.

The below debug shows a phase 1 negotiation failing because the two sides do not agree upon the attributes used.

```
#debug crypto isakmp

.Feb 25 17:38:48.486: ISAKMP:(0):Checking ISAKMP transform 0 against
priority 10 policy
.Feb 25 17:38:48.486: ISAKMP:        life type in seconds
.Feb 25 17:38:48.486: ISAKMP:        life duration (basic) of 3600
.Feb 25 17:38:48.486: ISAKMP:        encryption AES-CBC
.Feb 25 17:38:48.486: ISAKMP:        hash SHA
.Feb 25 17:38:48.486: ISAKMP:        auth pre-share
.Feb 25 17:38:48.486: ISAKMP:        default group 14
.Feb 25 17:38:48.486: ISAKMP:        keylength of 256
```

.Feb 25 17:38:48.486: ISAKMP:(0):**Hash algorithm offered does not match policy!**

The next debug shows a phase 2 negotiation failing because the two sides do not agree upon the attributes used.

```
#debug crypto ipsec

Feb 25 18:00:12.633: ISAKMP:(1007): IPSec policy invalidated proposal
with error 256
Feb 25 18:00:12.633: ISAKMP:(1007): phase 2 SA policy not acceptable!
(local 50.74.110.93 remote 206.111.121.166)
Feb 25 18:00:12.633: ISAKMP: set new node 928355547 to QM_IDLE
Feb 25 18:00:12.633: ISAKMP:(1007):Sending NOTIFY PROPOSAL_NOT_CHOSEN
protocol 3
         spi 713444760, message ID = 928355547
```

Chapter 7 - Security

Network security is a hot issue today, with cyber attacks reaching record levels across all sectors. It is important for any organization big or small to apply appropriate security practices.

TIP
Some great sources for security knowledge are the *Cisco Guide to Harden Cisco IOS Devices* and the *NSA Router Security Configuration Guide*, both of which are available for free on the web.

I'll be going over some of the topics covered in the above texts, but there is a great wealth of knowledge covering this ever changing and expanding topic. This is just the launching point for your security guidelines!

Security Best Practices

Below are some examples of simple steps you can take to harden your devices.

Secrets vs Passwords

By default passwords stored in configuration files are unencrypted. To encrypt these passwords enable the password-encryption service.

```
(config)#service password-encryption
```

Unfortunately, password-encryption offers weak protection. When entering passwords, remember to use the secret keyword rather than the password keyword. This tells the router to use a stronger encryption algorithm than the one used by `service password-encryption` on the stored passwords.

```
(config)# enable secret mypassword
(config)# username zzz secret mypassword02
```

Login Privilege Levels

When creating users on Cisco IOS devices, it is possible to set the default privilege level. To make it more difficult for attackers to gain access, change the default privilege level to 0, requiring them to type the enable password before making any changes to the system.

```
(config)#username peter privilege 0 secret mysecretpassword
```

Login Banner

Its a good idea to have a login banner on your routers and switches to solidify the access policy.

This command sets a login banner that is shown before logging into the device via ssh or telnet. The * is the specified character which must be entered to complete the input of the banner message, it can be any character you like.

```
(config)#banner login *
```

Security Services to Enable

The tcp-keepalives-in and tcp-keepalives-out commands monitor incoming and outgoing TCP connections to the router and automatically kill connections if no responses are received from the remote device. This helps mitigate attacks attempting to lock you out of the device.

```
(config)#service tcp-keepalives-in
(config)#service tcp-keepalives-out
```

Ip source routing allows a packet to specify how it wishes to be routed through a network. This can allow a hacker to bypass security mechanisms. To disable source routing use the following command:

```
(config)#no ip source-route
```

Setting DNS and NTP Servers

By default, Cisco devices will broadcast DNS requests out to their local subnets (255.255.255.255) to find a DNS server, but if they do not find one they will be unable to perform host translation. These broadcasts are dangerous - anyone listening in on the network can see these DNS requests!

To set the default DNS server use the command below. In this example we are using Google's Public DNS servers.

```
(config)#ip name-server 8.8.8.8 8.8.4.4
```

Having the correct time is required for most authentication schemes, and makes troubleshooting with log files so much easier. NTP sets the system clock to the correct time in UTC. In the example below I am using the pool.ntp.org project's servers.

```
(config)#ntp server pool.ntp.org
```

To check the current time, use the #show clock command.

Login Rate Limiting

It is important to prevent unauthorised access to your devices. Make it more difficult for attackers to brute force your passwords by locking out users after a certain number of incorrect attempts using the (config)# login command.

```
(config)#login block-for 120 attempts 5 within 100
```

The example above blocks login attempts for 120 Seconds if there are 5 login attempts within 100 seconds

Disabling unneeded services

Disabling unnecessary services is always a good security practice. The more services the device is running, the more potential security holes. Most people have no need of these services but they are enabled by default. Decide if you need these services, and if not disable them with the commands below.

Disables legacy service, PAD X.25
```
(config)#no service pad
```

Disables small servers
```
(config)#no service tcp-small-servers
(config)#no service udp-small-servers
```

Disables finger protocol
```
(config)#no ip finger
```

Disables loading configurations over the network during boot
```
(config)#no service config
(config)#no boot host dhcp
```

Turn off VTP if its not needed
```
(config)#vtp mode off
```

CDP and LLDP are powerful tools for mapping your network - for you, or your attackers. Consider turning them off if they are not needed. You can always turn them back on for troubleshooting.

Turn off Cisco Discovery Protocol (CDP) if its not needed
```
(config)#no cdp run
```

Disable Link Layer Discovery Protocol (LLDP) if its not needed
```
(config)#no lldp run
```

Many IOS devices can be programmed via a web gui, you can disable this gui with the following commands:

Disables the HTTP management server
```
(config)#no ip http server
```

Disables the HTTPS management server
```
(config)#no ip http secure-server
```

Interface Security

The following interface commands prevents your device from generating responses to several types of messages. This helps prevent an attacker from learning information about your network through scanning.

The no ip unreachables command prevents the generation of ICMP unreachable messages, no ip redirect prevents ICMP redirect messages, and no ip proxy-arp prevents responding to any arp messages which are not the interface's IP address.

```
(config-if)#no ip unreachables
(config-if)#no ip redirect
(config-if)#no ip proxy-arp
```

Routing Protocol Authentication

Routing protocols such as EIGRP and OSPF support optional authentication mechanisms, making sure routers can only share routing information with other authorised routers. This can typically be done with pre shared keys or MD5 hashes. Hashes are considered much more secure, and should be preferred over PSKs.

Using authentication helps prevents malicious attackers from manipulating your routing protocols. Check out the Cisco documentation on your routing protocol for the specifics on how to enable authentication.

SNMP Monitoring

It is very important to have a strong monitoring solution in place on your network, to help better understand and search traffic flows, resource usage, and security breaches.

Several monitoring applications exist from commercial offering such as Solarwinds NCM, to open source applications such as Nagios and Cacti.

To monitor your devices, enable Simple Network Management Protocol (SNMP) on your devices. It is a good idea to change the community name from the default (public) and to apply a network ACL to limit who can poll the SNMP server.

```
(config)#snmp-server community mycommunitystring RO 1
```

In the command above, the number "1" represents the ACL of allowed hosts, and RO is the access type (Read Only). The server can also be configured in RW (Read/Write) mode if you would like to send commands via SNMP Traps.

Using a Syslog Server

It is a best practice to backup your cisco log files to a secure location. By default, these files are erased upon reboot. These files can be invaluable in troubleshooting or for post attack forensics.

There are many log servers available, from commercial offerings such as Splunk and Kiwi to open source programs such as syslogd.

To send logs to a syslog server use the logging command:

```
(config)#logging 10.120.61.103
```

You may want to change the default logging level to something less verbose. There are a total of 7 logging levels, with 5 and up being logged to file by default.

```
(config)#logging trap 4
```

Level	Description
0 - emergency	System unusable
1 - alert	Immediate action needed
2 - critical	Critical condition
3 - error	Error condition
4 - warning	Warning condition
5 - notification	Normal but significant condition
6 - informational	Informational message only
7 - debugging	Appears during debugging only

Access Control Lists (ACLs)

Access control lists are lists that define permissions to specific locations. They can be used to deny/grant access to/from a certain IP address or port. ACL's are not just used for traffic filtering, they are also used for traffic classification.

There are two major types of ACLs, standard and extended. **Standard ACLs** permit or deny access by ip address only. **Extended ACLs** permit or deny access by protocol, ip address, and port number.

Standard ACLs are numbered 1-99 and 1300-1999, Extended ACLs are numbered 100-199 and 2000-2699. Numbers are not always needed, as it is possible to create named ACLs as well.

TIP
It is important to note that rules in an ACL are followed sequentially and the first line that matches the traffic is processed so its recommended to put more specific rules near the top of the ACL, and more general rules near the bottom. There is an implicit "deny all" statement at the end of every ACL, meaning if there are no matches in the list the traffic is denied.

ACLs must be applied to an interface for either inbound or outbound traffic. An inbound ACL pertains to all traffic received by the interface. An outbound ACL pertains to all traffic sent by the interface. You can only have one inbound and one outbound ACL per interface.

Standard ACL Example

Below is the syntax of a standard ACL. It begins with the keyword access-list followed by a number which is used to reference this list. Next, the action is specified - permit or deny. After that is the address to which the rule applies and the wildcard mask used to specify multiple addresses.

```
(config)# access-list {1-99} {permit | deny} source-addr [source-
wildcard]
```

The example below permits all traffic from 10.0.0.0/24.

```
(config)# access-list 1 permit 10.0.0.0 0.0.0.255
```

Extended ACL Example

Below is the syntax for Extended ACLs. Like standard ACLs you must specify a number followed by permit or deny. Next you specify the Transport Layer protocol used such as ICMP, TCP, UDP, or GRE. After that you specify both the source and destination address, using wildcard masks to specify multiple addresses. In the case of TCP or UDP traffic you can also specify the port number and other attributes as well.

```
(config)# access-list {100-199} {permit | deny} protocol source-addr
[source-wildcard] [operator operand] destination-addr [destination-
wildcard] [operator operand] [established]
```

The first example below permits ICMP packets from 172.16.0.0/16 to any destination.

```
access-list 101 permit icmp 172.16.0.0 0.0.255.255 any
```

The second example permits SMTP traffic from 10.0.0.0/24 to 192.168.0.0/16.

```
access-list 150 permit tcp 10.0.0.0 0.0.0.255 192.168.0.0 0.0.255.255
eq 25
```

Modifying ACLs

The above examples used the `(config)#access-list` command for creating ACLs, but below I'll show the `(config)# ip access-list` command. They are very similar, the difference being `(config)# ip access-list` puts you into ACL editing mode, where it is not necessary to start each line with something like `(config)# access-list 110` ! So the `(config)# ip access-list` can be easier for entering large ACLs, because it requires less typing!

TIP
You can create named access lists with the `(config)# ip access-list extended` *name* command. They behave just like other ACLs, but are easier to remember.

TIP
The remark command allows entering comments into the list. They show up in the config, but not in the `#show access-list` command.

```
(config)# ip access-list extended 110
(config-ext-nacl)#  remark Allow HTTP
(config-ext-nacl)#  permit tcp any any eq 80
(config-ext-nacl)#  remark Allow HTTPS
(config-ext-nacl)#  permit tcp any any eq 443
(config-ext-nacl)#  remark Allow HTTP Alt
(config-ext-nacl)#  permit tcp any any eq 8080
(config-ext-nacl)#  remark Allow DNS
(config-ext-nacl)#  permit tcp any any eq 53
(config-ext-nacl)#  remark Allow DNS
(config-ext-nacl)#  permit udp any any eq 53
(config-ext-nacl)#  remark Allow NTP
(config-ext-nacl)#  permit tcp any any eq 123
(config-ext-nacl)#  remark Allow NTP
(config-ext-nacl)#  permit udp any any eq 123
(config-ext-nacl)#  remark Allow IRC
(config-ext-nacl)#  permit tcp any any range 6660 6670
(config-ext-nacl)#  remark Allow IRC
(config-ext-nacl)#  permit tcp any any eq 7000
```

To show the access list, use the `#show access-list 110` command, where 110 is the acl number.

Notice the line numbers in the ACL - 10,20,30,etc. These numbers allow you to add new lines into the ACL at specific locations. For example, I can add a new line at line 1 using the command below. The preceding 1 means enter this statement at line number 1.

```
(config)# ip access-list extended 110
(config-ext-nacl)#1 deny ip any 1.1.1.1 255.255.255.255
```

```
COM4 - PuTTY                                                    — □ X
wr000netsw01#
wr000netsw01#
wr000netsw01#
wr000netsw01#
wr000netsw01#
wr000netsw01#
wr000netsw01#
wr000netsw01#
wr000netsw01#
wr000netsw01#
wr000netsw01#
wr000netsw01#show access-lists 110
Extended IP access list 110
    1 deny ip any host 1.1.1.1
   10 permit tcp any any eq www
   20 permit tcp any any eq 443
   30 permit tcp any any eq 8080
   40 permit tcp any any eq domain
   50 permit udp any any eq domain
   60 permit tcp any any eq 123
   70 permit udp any any eq ntp
   80 permit tcp any any range 6660 6670
   90 permit tcp any any eq 7000
wr000netsw01#
```

To renumber the ACL to start at 10 and increase in increments of 10, use the `(config)#ip`
`access-list resequence 110 10 10` command.

ACL Labs

ACLs can be used to secure access to your devices. For example, applying inbound ACLs to
the VTY lines prevents unauthorised users from SSHing into your devices.

Lab 1

This example allows SSH access from only a select group of IPs, such as your office or
datacenter external IP addresses.

The "access-class 1" in command specifies that traffic matching ACL 1 is allowed, all other
traffic is denied.

TIP
Its important to note that VTY lines use the `(config-line)#access-class` command
instead of the `(config-if)#access-group` command used on interfaces.

```
(config)#access-list 1 permit 61.104.226.128 0.0.0.31
(config)#access-list 1 permit 63.38.232.224 0.0.0.15
```

```
(config)#access-list 1 permit 68.163.56.144 0.0.0.15
!
(config)#line vty 0 15
(config-line)#transport input ssh
(config-line)#access-class 1 in
```

Lab 2

This example creates an ACL to prevent your Cisco device from responding to ping requests.

We will use ACL 101 to specify the external IP addresses/ranges which should be permitted to ping and then explicitly block any ICMP traffic from elsewhere to the IP address of the Cisco device (207.239.120.231). Lastly we apply the ACL inbound on the interface.

```
(config)#access-list 101 permit icmp 166.104.226.128 0.0.0.31 any
(config)#access-list 101 permit icmp 65.38.232.224 0.0.0.15 any
(config)#access-list 101 permit icmp 61.163.56.144 0.0.0.15 any
(config)#access-list 101 deny icmp any host 207.239.120.231
(config)#access-list 101 permit ip any any
!
(config)#int gi 0/1
(config-if)#ip access-group 1 in
```

Lab 3

Sometimes its necessary to have isolated VLANs on your Layer 3 switches. For example, if you have a guest wireless network, or a network for vendor equipment. To make sure this vlan cannot communicate with other VLANs, a simple ACL can be used.

The example below prevents any ip traffic on a vlan 10 from communicating with any private ip address space in use in your network. All traffic to public IPs is allowed, however.

```
(config)#access-list 101 deny ip any 10.0.0.0 0.255.255.255
(config)#access-list 101 deny ip any 192.168.0.0 0.0.255.255
(config)#access-list 101 deny ip any 172.16.0.0 0.15.255.255
(config)#access-list 101 permit ip any any
!
(config)#vlan 10
(config)#ip access-group 101 in
```

Context-Based Access Control (CBAC)

Stateful vs Stateless Firewalls

Access Control Lists are useful tools, but they are stateless "firewalls" in design. Stateless firewalls block or allow traffic based on static values, such as source or destination address. They are unaware of traffic flows, meaning they are relatively easy to trick through crafting bogus packets.

Stateful Firewalls in contrast are aware of traffic flows, they store the state of traffic flowing across them. This allows them to make more intelligent decisions such as only allowing traffic that is associated with an active connection.

CBAC Configuration

CBAC is a method to perform stateful firewalling with cisco routers. It works through enabling traffic inspection, allowing the router to keep track of state information.

To configure CBAC, you must first enable IP inspection for certain protocols globally using the `(config)#ip inspect name` *name protocol* command.

Next, you must add the inspection group to your interfaces. Use the `(config)#ip inspect name in/out` command for this. Out is used on the external interface, and in is used on the internal interface.

CBAC LAB

In this example we are going to use CBAC to deny access from a location, but to permit traffic to it. Meaning sessions established from site A to site B are allowed in, but site B cannot speak to site A otherwise. In the example below, gi0/0 is the external interface, and gi0/1 is the internal interface.

The access list prevents traffic from 10.0.0.0/13 from accessing the local network unless the traffic was sourced from the local network. That's the advantage of stateful firewalls!

```
(config)#ip inspect name test tcp
(config)#ip inspect name test udp
(config)#ip inspect name test http
(config)#ip inspect name test https
(config)#ip inspect name test icmp
!
(config)#access-list 151 deny ip 10.0.0.0 0.3.255.255 any
(config)#access-list 151 permit ip any any
!
(config)#int gi0/0
```

```
(config-if)#ip inspect test out
!
(config)#int gi0/1
(config-if)#ip inspect test in
(config-if)#ip access-group 151 out
```

Conclusion

Over the course of this book we have covered basic cisco configurations, advanced features, switching, routing, WAN technologies, and security topics. I hope that the information was as useful to you as it was to me in my early career.

I invite you to provide feedback on this book -- more tips, content suggestions, or pointing out any errors.

Thank you so much for reading!

Appendix - Full Example Configurations

IPsec Tunnel Example

```
!
hostname Test2 !set hostname
enable secret enable
service password-encryption !encrypted passwords in configs
service tcp-keepalives-in !kill timed out sessions inbound
service tcp-keepalives-out !kill timed out sessions outbound
no service tcp-small-servers !disable unneeded services
no service udp-small-servers !disable unneeded services
no ip http server !turn off http configuration server
no ip http secure-server !turn off https configuration server
no ip source-route !do not allow hosts to specify routes
!
ip name-server 8.8.8.8 8.8.4.4 !set google DNS for name server
ntp server pool.ntp.org !set ntp.org as time server
login block-for 100 attempts 5 within 100
logging buffered 4096 !set logging buffer to 4MB
no service pad !disable unneeded service
no ip finger !disable unneeded service
no service config !no auto loading of config files over the network
no boot host dhcp !no  autoloading of config files over the network
logging trap 4 !set logging level
!
aaa new-model !enables aaa
aaa authentication login default local !sets auth mode to local
ip domain name example.com !sets the domain name
crypto key generate rsa modulus 2048
IP SSH version 2 !enables ssh v2
ip scp server enable !enables scp
username root privilege 15 secret root
!
line vty 0 15 !configures virtual terminal lines
transport input ssh !specifies ssh only
exit
!
interface GigabitEthernet0/0 !external interface
```

```
no shutdown
ip address 50.74.110.93 255.255.255.248
crypto map mymap !apply crypto map to external interface
no ip unreachables !does not generate ICMP unreachable packets
no ip redirect !does not generate ICMP redirect packets
no ip proxy-arp !disables proxy arp
!
interface GigabitEthernet0/1
!internal interface
no shutdown
ip address 192.168.20.1 255.255.255.0
no ip unreachables
no ip redirect
no ip proxy-arp
!
ip route 0.0.0.0 0.0.0.0 50.74.110.89
!
crypto isakmp policy 10
encryption aes 256 !isakmp encryption
hash sha256 !isakmp hash
auth pre-share  !isakmp auth type
group 14 !diffie hellman group
exit
!
crypto isakmp key testkey address 206.111.121.166 !sets PSK and peer
!
!defines phase 2 attributes, ESP Mode, AES 256, SHA
crypto ipsec transform-set myset esp-aes 256 esp-sha-hmac
exit
!
access-list 101 permit ip 192.168.0.0 0.0.255.255 10.0.0.0
0.255.255.255
access-list 101 permit ip 192.168.0.0 0.0.255.255 192.168.0.0
0.0.255.255
access-list 101 permit ip 192.168.0.0 0.0.255.255 172.16.0.0
0.15.255.255
!
crypto map mymap 10 ipsec-isakmp
 set peer 206.111.121.166 !peer ip address
 set transform-set myset
 match address 101 !addresses allowed over VPN
exit
!
```

GRE over IPSEC Example

```
!
hostname Test1 !set hostname
enable secret enable
service password-encryption !encrypted passwords in configs
service tcp-keepalives-in !kill timed out sessions inbound
service tcp-keepalives-out !kill timed out sessions outbound
no service tcp-small-servers !disable unneeded services
no service udp-small-servers !disable unneeded services
no ip http server !turn off http configuration server
no ip http secure-server !turn off https configuration server
no ip source-route !do not allow hosts to specify routes
!
ip name-server 8.8.8.8 8.8.4.4 !set google DNS for name server
ntp server pool.ntp.org !set ntp.org as time server
login block-for 100 attempts 5 within 100
logging buffered 4096 !set logging buffer to 4MB
no service pad !disable unneeded service
no ip finger !disable unneeded service
no service config !no auto loading of config files over the network
no boot host dhcp !no  autoloading of config files over the network
logging trap 4 !set logging level
!
aaa new-model !enables aaa
aaa authentication login default local !sets auth mode to local
ip domain name example.com !sets the domain name
crypto key generate rsa modulus 2048
IP SSH version 2 !enables ssh v2
ip scp server enable !enables scp
username root privilege 15 secret root
!
line vty 0 15 !configures virtual terminal lines
transport input ssh !specifies ssh only
exit
!
interface GigabitEthernet0/0
no shutdown
crypto map mymap !apply crypto map to external interface
ip address 50.74.110.93 255.255.255.248
no ip unreachables !does not generate ICMP unreachable packets
no ip redirect !does not gnerate ICMP redirect packets
no ip proxy-arp !disables proxy arp
!
interface GigabitEthernet0/1
```

```
no shutdown
ip address 192.168.20.1 255.255.255.0
no ip unreachables
no ip redirect
no ip proxy-arp
!
interface Tunnel1
ip address 172.16.0.2 255.255.255.0 !gre tunnel interface
tunnel source gi0/0 !sources traffic from external interface
tunnel destination 206.111.121.166
!destination is the peer's external ip
!
crypto isakmp policy 10 !defines phase 1 attributes
encryption aes 256 !using AES 256 cypher
hash sha256 !using SHA 256 hashing algorthim
auth pre-share !using PSKs
group 14 !using diffie-hellman group 14 2048bit
!
crypto isakmp key testkey address 206.111.121.166 !sets PSK and peer
!
!defines phase 2 attributes, ESP Mode, AES 256, SHA
crypto ipsec transform-set myset esp-aes 256 esp-sha-hmac
mode transport !sets transport mode IPsec
!
crypto map mymap 10 ipsec-isakmp
set peer 206.111.121.166 !peer IP address
set transform-set myset
match address vpnendpoints                              !allows
all addresses over VPN
!
ip route 0.0.0.0 0.0.0.0 50.74.110.89
ip route 192.168.10.0 255.255.255.0 172.16.0.1              !route
traffic to remote network via peer's tunnel address
!
ip access-list extended vpnendpoints
permit gre any any
!
```